Driving Your Destiny

Taking Control of Your Career and Living Goals

Published in England
by GWiz Publishing

Oakhurst, Mardens Hill, Crowborough, Sussex. TN6 1XL. UK.
Tel (+44) 1892 309205

info@gwiztraining.com

www.gwiztraining.com

First published 2020.
10 9 8 7 6 5 4 3 2 1

ISBN: 978-0-9955979-5-2

Contents (Big Picture Bits)

Bits

Contents (Specific Pieces)

Foreword

You are now reading a book of 'Bits and Pieces'... a book of thoughts, reflections, tools, tips, models, concepts, techniques, processes, questions, philosophies, mindsets…

Here, you will discover 'things to explore'; hundreds of practical applications, developed over a quarter of a century from working with tens of thousands of individuals. For this reason, the material herein is mostly mine, and where it is not mine originally (or it is a development of someone else's work), I have endeavoured to give credit in the notes section.

Driving Your Destiny is designed to provoke your thinking, to inspire you and help you to take action that will get you the results you want in your career and life.

And let me give you a warning up front…

Nothing in this book is true…
Nothing in this book is right or correct!

Without taking anything away from our explorations, the tips and advice in this book are simply my experience (direct and drawn from many others). Whilst the ideas have been pretty well tested, they are not the *only* way of getting in the driving seat! If they work for you as they are written, then that is brilliant! I recommend, however, that you seek to adapt some of the content into your own style. For example, when I use phrases like '*You could say*: *XYZ*', remember that these are examples... so please do not use them as a script! Find your own way and your own voice... otherwise I (as the author) am in the driving seat of *your* life and career... and that really would *not* do!

How to navigate this book

Because the title is 'Driving Your Destiny' it seemed appropriate to give you a range of different ways of working through and around the Bits and Pieces:

1. You can easily ***read the book cover to cover***. In general, there is a logical flow from start to finish.
2. You can ***dip in***... treat it like a book of random ideas... turn to a page and discover...
3. You can ***work from the Contents (Specific Pieces) pages*** and see what appeals.
4. You can ***use the 'What's Your Outcome?' page*** that highlights specific concerns, questions, challenges and needs you might have at a given moment in time.
5. You can ***have a look at the index*** and look for interconnected themes of interest.
6. You can ***pick your own path***! When you read a specific piece, you will find a box at the end with some new options (of connected pieces) for exploration. In this way you can take a journey through the book, driving your own destiny as you go!

And if you still have questions, perhaps situations not fully addressed or a desire for clarification, feel free to contact me!

What is your Outcome?

You would like to:	Read Pieces:
Get better at connecting with others	5, 7, 52, 55, 91
Enhance your confidence	6, 28, 47, 75
Improve your success at interviews	70, 94
Approach networking in a more positive way	101, 105
Get a better grip on your career	17, 109, 123
Focus on your higher purpose	31, 35, 74
Feel happier, on top and more in control	42, 111
Deal with blocks to your career	37, 114
Motivate yourself	9, 83, 124
Take control of your own life	2, 20, 107
Create more opportunities to show what you can do	14, 53, 89
Set goals that take you in the right direction	21, 30
Find a company you like working for	36, 62, 81
Progress, step up the ladder, get a promotion	51, 65
Develop a better work-life balance	41, 108
Be more influential and persuasive	19, 57
Better handle change and uncertainty	87, 119, 122
Understand where you might have been going wrong	22, 35, 50, 67, 72
Make a good impression	56, 63, 80, 92
Get noticed!	84, 86
Out of work, looking for work	10, 17, 93, 96, 101, 124

The Introductory Bit

Pieces About The Book

1. Now is the Time...

In the beginning... I grew up in an 'Older Folks Home'. Not because I am doing the whole thing backwards (like Benjamin Button), but because my parents ran a residential home for the elderly during the first ten-years of my life.

The place was called Downsvale, and as a child (with child logic), it seemed that there were two types of folk at the home:

1) There were those that told me I was lucky to have all the opportunities I had... that *they* never had. They spoke of *wishing* they had done things. Generally, their main interest appeared to be: "what time's tea?" They would also tell me off for running around, so I tended to avoid them where possible. Perhaps I was being unfair, but I *was* only 7!

2) And then there were those who spoke of things they had done during their lives... amazing tales of where they had been and what they had got up to. They were children in the Edwardian era, when (for example) motor cars began to make an appearance and the Victorian spirit of adventure was becoming more accessible to more people. These folks were still bright eyed and bushy tailed, staying current with events and modern times. These were the folk I spent more time with... because they spoke about the things that they were *glad* they had done.

And that was the difference I noticed: "I wish I..." vs "I'm glad I..." I knew then, that when I reached my Downsvale moment in life, I wanted to be able to look back and say: "I'm glad I did...".

And of course, now is the time to begin to make those things happen that one day *you* will be looking back and being glad that you did!

And here you discover the purpose of the book you are reading... because ***now*** *is the time... to begin to* ***make those things happen****... that one day...* ***you will be glad*** *you did!*

To explore 'purpose'... 31
To overcome a lack of personal direction... 124
Or continue to get in the Driving Seat...

2. *The Driving Seat*

I have worked with tens of thousands of people during my career. Some seemed a bit lost, others seemed 'sorted' and some were in the middle there, floating about between the two ends.

Those that seemed 'sorted' interested me. What made them so different to the others? The metaphor that made sense to me was that they were 'in the driving seat' of their own experience, their own career and their own destiny. Of course, they faced pot-holes, road blocks, jams and set-backs… but they were better able to adjust and correct their course.

The lost spirits seemed to be in the passenger seat (or perhaps even in the *back* seat). They *waited* for someone to notice them, to drive them, to spoon-feed them… and then they would sometimes complain about the way they were being driven and/or where they had ended up.

Being in the driving seat means taking responsibility for your life and career experience. It means *both* <u>managing your expectations</u> *and* <u>managing your reality</u>. When we do this effectively, we frame the experiences we have, see, hear and feel… and we take action to make things better in our lives. We feel more in control of our destiny.

At extreme, being in the driving seat also relates to our motivation and determination: think of something in the past that you *really* wanted… and then you got that thing or made it happen. Consider your single mindedness in 'bringing it into existence'. Whatever it took, you would seek opportunities and were ready to do whatever it took to get that thing or to make it happen. *Nothing* could stop you.

Of course, we might be single-minded to the point of losing other things (e.g. a relationship). Perhaps that does not matter to you... but if it does, then being in the driving seat means taking *everything into account* and finding a way to reach your goals *and* maintain (or indeed strengthen) your relationships.

To explore a few more metaphors, when you are in the driving seat:

- you tend to feel on top of things, you are able to surf the choppy waters, stay afloat if knocked off and then get back on board,
- you get back in the saddle if the horse throws you,
- you remain 'at cause' (rather than 'at effect'[i]), able to take responsibility for yourself, your feelings and your actions... you respond rather than react[ii],
- you 'bounce back'!

And that is what this book is about... taking control of your career... being ready for the opportunities when they arise.

To explore the language of goal motivations... 23
To understand why some people do not progress... 67
Or continue to the Resilient Career...

3. The Resilient Career

Things change… and life throws curveballs and googlies at us. We may, at times, have to deal with doubt, uncertainty, dilemmas, obstacles, brick walls, challenges and seemingly insurmountable problems[i].

Having a resilient[ii] career means (over your lifetime) being open to working with different companies and industries, doing more than one job, indeed different types of jobs… and maybe even a mix of employed and self-employed.

When I was in my early teens, I was given some advice by a friend of my parents: in life, you can either earn money (work for others) or make money (work for yourself)! There are pros and cons to being employed and being self-employed. I think, in reality, that there is a spectrum of possibilities between the two. Being a consultant or interim, for example, seems to be somewhere along that continuum.

To build a resilient career means, for example:

- To have goals, strategies and back-up plans
- To be able to communicate your needs and be empathetic to others
- To reality check… converting dreams into practical actions
- To stay mentally healthy in the face of adversity
- To develop your self-esteem, valuing yourself **and** others
- To understand and then maintain your boundaries

- To remain as objective as possible, rather than taking things personally
- To understand yourself, your drivers, your values and your beliefs
- To hold a 'growth mindset[iii]' with the ability to adapt, learn and improve
- To stay focussed and motivated whilst looking for work during times of unemployment

And that is what this book is about... helping you to strengthen your understanding of what you will need... to take responsibility for yourself and to develop flexible approaches in making your career your own.

To understand your values... 34
To explore resilience further... 40
Or continue to what drives success...

The First Bit

Pieces About Success

4. *What Drives Success?*

Having studied highly-effective influencers for the past few decades, there appears to be four key areas to personal success:

- Connection
- Credibility
- Flexibility
- Persistence

Of course, there may be more, and you will no doubt discover them on your journey; however, this is a useful set of descriptions to begin with.

Connection is… your likeability, your capacity to build rapport with other people so that they enjoy being in your company. When we like someone, we are more likely to want to work with them.

Credibility is… your ability to build trust. It is based on qualities like your authority (including your voice and demeanour), your experience, your qualifications and your confidence.

Flexibility is… your ability to adapt to whatever the environment throws at you. Rather than having only one way of doing things, you might have seven or eight!

Persistence is… your ability to get back in the driving seat after a rejection, a difficult problem or when the situation gets uncomfortable.

You can develop all of these success factors... and I encourage you to do so.

Remember though... just because you may have all four factors working for you does not mean you are 'right' or that you hold the moral high-ground. There are many top leaders out there in the world who have developed these qualities, but it would be hard to congratulate them for their ethical stance.

With the four qualities combined comes potential power and with that comes responsibility.

In essence, this whole book is designed to help you develop and enhance your connection, credibility, flexibility and persistence.

To increase your luck... 12
To explore the foundations of persuasion... 57
Or continue to connection...

5. Connection

Some people are easy to get on with. They are friendly, often smiling and laughing, and they make you feel better for having met them. The second time you meet them, even if you don't remember their name, you get a warm, positive feeling!

How do you become one of these 'connectors'? Here are some key factors and behaviours:

- **Give Empathy**: Show empathy for others. If they are in a 'positive', constructive state (e.g. proud of something they have achieved), show that you are happy for them. If they are in a 'negative', destructive state (e.g. angry or upset), show that you are concerned for them. Where possible, reassure them that how they are feeling is understandable and 'normal'. In addition, acknowledge their position or perspective (even if you don't necessarily share it). For example, you might say; "That must be tough," but avoid: "I know how you feel"!
- **Get Empathy**: Sometimes, it can be helpful to 'pull' empathy from others. For example, you might say: "Put yourself in my shoes… how would you feel if… how would *you* handle the situation…"
- **Show you are on the same side**: Where possible, demonstrate that you have shared goals, values, aims and vision with the people you are talking to. If you are proposing an idea, make sure to show how it fits *their* plans, objectives and interests rather than just your own.
- **Involve others**: Involve others in your ideas, plans, solutions and decisions. Ask others for their advice and input. Appeal to their knowledge and expertise… ask

questions *and* listen. Where possible, add their input into your plans and let them know! People don't tend to reject their own ideas. If they were involved, they are more likely to get on board with you.

- **Keep your humour**: When appropriate, find moments of humour, light-heartedness, laughter and smiles. Demonstrate enthusiasm for the ideas of others... and cheerfulness for simply being alive!

Of course, we could go over the top with any of the above... and that could become irritating to others. Read the situation and the folk that are there.

All in all, how do you want to be perceived? As someone who is unapproachable and self-centred... or as someone who is interested in and genuinely cares about others?

To understand what makes and breaks rapport... 56
To connect with the 'right people'... 88
Or continue to credibility...

6. Credibility

Some people you meet will have an easy confidence about them, neither arrogant nor apologetic for their existence. They come across with a degree of authority in their subject and seem well worth listening too. We are glad to have them on board (e.g. a project). They make us feel safe… that we are in good hands. They are trustworthy, keeping promises and not letting us down. They usually admit to mistakes (with a view to learning from those mistakes and correcting them) and are comfortable enough to admit when they do not have an answer…

Here are some key qualities and behaviours that will enhance your credibility.

- **Develop your confidence**: Confidence and strong self-esteem (*not* arrogance), demonstrates you are credible and comfortable in your own boots. Be prepared to introduce and present yourself when appropriate. Communicate your expertise through your job title, number of years, research, qualifications…
- **Be clear**: Whenever you communicate, be clear and concise. Where appropriate, set expectations and provide a structure or an agenda. Clarify agreements… who is doing what, by when etc. Keep others in the loop and request they keep you in the loop too.
- **Make decisions**: Be prepared to make a decision, even if you have to re-decide at a later date. Let people know why you have made the decision and, during uncertain times, the likelihood of having to remake the decision when new data presents itself.

- **Stay true to your core**: It is easier to be honest, congruent and consistent when you make decisions and take actions according your values and principles. Hence, *get clear* about your own values, mission, purpose and principles!
- **Prepare and Present**: Whenever you present information, in whatever form, give evidence and examples to demonstrate you have thought it through. Make sure any outcomes or objectives have a measurable and 'concrete' end result. If necessary, show your audience a printed version of what you are saying (for some folks this makes it more definite and believable!)
- **Dress to impress**: Remember that what you wear creates an impression. Think about other people you meet… are they professional or casual, smart or scruffy, memorable or non-descript? What does this tell you about them?
- **Act with certainty**: Develop a voice of certainty and strong body-language signals. The person who is the most certain in a specific situation is likely to be the most persuasive[i]. Speak with authority… **and** be prepared to discuss alternatives. You don't have to be 'right', *you just need to be confident* in your own ideas. Those with credibility are prepared to admit they are wrong or that there is a better idea or they don't know or they are sorry for something… and they do it with grace and with confidence!

To address Imposter Syndrome…78
To be seen and heard in meetings… 84
Or continue to connection and credibility…

7. Connection and Credibility

Although it is possible to be successful via either connection or credibility, you will increase your odds dramatically as you develop *both.* Connection and credibility are in the mind of the audience, i.e. how likeably, trustworthy, ethical and authoritative they perceive you to be. You may believe you are all of these things… but you will only have an impact if others believe them too.

Some folks are very friendly and likable… the 'people' people! However, they can come across as non-assertive or as a joker… and hence not be taken seriously. Other folks may be very credible… a real expert in their field. You may trust them, but you wouldn't want to work with them. Perhaps they come across as arrogant, aggressive, distant, aloof or unapproachable.

How long do you think it takes to build ***connection*** with someone? The answer… it depends! It appears that there are 'layers' of rapport and hence likeability develops over time. However, studies on 'impressions' suggest that the first layer of connection happens immediately. And at that point we make a decision (probably primal): is this person friend or foe? Do I like them, yes or no? After our initial judgement, we then *seek to confirm our initial judgement*[i]. If we like the person straight away, we continue to look for what we like. If we are not so sure, we continue to look for what we do not like. Alas… we do indeed judge the book by its cover!

What about ***credibility*** and trust… surely that takes more time? Apparently not. It is that same as connection. There is an initial, immediate assessment and then layers of trust building after that. From research on first impressions, we also make a judgement about a person's confidence, competence and honesty... and all within two seconds[ii]!

So, do whatever you can to make sure your first impressions are positively favourable ones.

Be purposeful at first contact... get on the right track... and then the rest will be easier.

To understand the assertive you... 52
To establish your legacy... 74
Or continue to flexibility...

8. Flexibility

The person within a system who has the greatest flexibility is the most likely to survive and thrive over a period of time[i].

To be flexible means to be adaptable, to have a range of approaches in a given situation and to be able to innovate when faced with new and different circumstances.

When someone has only one way of dealing with a situation, it will work… sometimes! But having three or more options gives you choice. It also means that if your first approach is not working, you have back-up plans.

Indeed, the more strategies you have for handling specific situations, the more confident you will feel. Consider some areas of life where you are really confident. If something isn't working quite right, you will have other ways of handling the situation.

As well as having a range of actions you could take, flexibility is also about your ability to think through and around situations… to be able to see things from a number of different perspectives.

When we can see something from only one perspective, our thinking becomes stuck and rigid. We are unable to empathise with others or 'put ourselves in their shoes'.

To be able to see things from multiple perspectives not only allows you to build rapport more easily with others, it helps you to manage your emotions and to be creative and innovative in your approach to solving problems.

It can help us to be more balanced, resilient and fair in our dealings with others when we understand that all we have is a perspective on (and not THE truth of) the situation.

How we frame and interpret things affects how we feel. I heard a story of two people having a conversation. One person was learning English as a second language and was trying to describe a turtle. Not knowing the word, he drew a turtle and the other person told him what it was. He wrote the word 'turtle' under the rough picture. They laughed together. A pleasant interaction. However, a third person overheard the end of the interaction and believed they were talking about him... drawing pictures of him, calling him a turtle and laughing at him. He immediately complained to the HR department. Who knows what went through the complainant's mind and what they had experienced in the past? However, if this was a regular 'interpretation filter' for them, life cannot have been much fun.

So, for your own success and wellbeing, practice interpreting or explaining events in a number of different ways!

To add flexibility to tough goals... 25
To discover how flexibility links with confidence... 75
Or continue to persistence...

9. Persistence

What do you do if your first approach does not work?

Too many people take it as rejection and give up. They say things like: "I've tried everything…" when really, they have not!

Imagine a small child taking their first steps. They pull themselves up, focus on their destination and set off… usually to fall down on their backside! So, they crawl back to a stable start point, pull themselves up… focus… and off they go again… until finally they get there. They don't think: "That didn't work, I'm not doing that again. I've tried everything… you'll have to carry me round for the rest of my life!"

Now imagine having the self-same tenacity that the small child has when they are learning to walk. Sheer determination. Total commitment! Unstoppable motivation. Splendid oomph and va-va-voom!

There is an old Latin proverb that I rather like… "Fortune favours the brave". It is well known… almost a cliché now… but it *can* become a powerful motivator. And in this instance, being brave means facing the possibility of barriers or of rejection or of not getting it right first time.

Here, we could be talking about a form of resilience. Getting back up when we get knocked down… and having another go.

How do you light the fire within… and how do you reignite the flame when others try to douse it? What do you do when life throws a bucket of water at you? How do you fire up the furnace, build up a head of steam and power the engine of locomotion? (I will stop with the metaphor now!)

How are you motivated? Do you motivate yourself or get motivation from others… or a mix of both? In general terms, the most powerful form of motivation is self-motivation… even when we like to get praise and recognition from others. If you are more motivated by what you get from others, but others are not around, imagine their thanks and the look on their face… that you have made a positive difference for them in some way.

Think back on times when you were totally motivated, when you had that inner resolve and 'single-mindedness'… when you were in flow and nothing could stop you. What was it that moved you so?

When I was about 12, there was a competition at school to win a rugby ball (signed by some international players). All we had to do was sell the most amount of tickets for a school fundraising rugby-match. I got it into my head that I wanted to win it and I ended up going door-to-door around our local streets after school. The result? I sold over 100 tickets (the next kid in the competition sold 18)! It was my first experience of 'sales-rejection' (as some people *literally* slammed the door in my face), but I really didn't care… I just wanted the rugby ball and I figured that the *next* house might just buy one or two more tickets towards my goal!

To get into a state of readiness… 14
To find out how to handle your 'inner critic'… 47
Or continue to the persistence/flexibility combo…

10. The Persistence/Flexibility Combo

Persistence, combined with flexibility, is a force to be reckoned with. Imagine someone who has a drive to make things happen. What do they do whenever they encounter an obstacle? Most times, they change their *course* rather than their *cause.*

When I have time, I like to drive down country roads to see where they go and where they come out. It is amazing how often this proves useful at a later date when there is a traffic jam on the main road!

Nature (the most successful and long-lasting 'living' thing on planet Earth) is full of examples of flexible persistence. The Theory of Evolution is a perfect example. How do species survive and thrive? By adapting and persevering. Indeed, each obstacle or setback tends to make the species 'stronger'.

Your brain is another beautiful example. It is learning, updating and making new connections all the time. Even when the brain is damaged, in many cases it has the capacity to rewire itself. This ability is known as neural plasticity[i]. If your brain is being flexible and persistent… there is no reason why the rest of you can't be!

We can develop our flexibility over time, particularly if we have the will to do so. The key to this is 'reflection'… and it really doesn't have to take long (i.e. we are not talking about long periods of 'naval gazing')!

If things don't go your way in any given situation, ask yourself:

- What could I do differently next time?

- And what else?

Remember, success is often a numbers game… of probabilities. Increase your odds by adapting to the situation, learning new ways not to do it and getting curious!

Develop a set of strategies for dealing with this situation in the future. And especially, strategies that you feel happy with, excited about and motivated by! A solution without enthusiasm is a chore, a sinking feeling… and we are less likely to implement it. And, for the same reason, make sure your strategies fit with your values!

Persistence and flexibility are especially essential if we are 'between jobs', i.e. unemployed and looking for work. Finding work can be a job in and of itself[ii].

Are you ready to be formidably formable, relentless in your ability to adjust, develop and evolve? And are you ready to think literally, laterally and round corners in your pursuit of resilience and determination?

To use nature as a metaphor for tenacity… 29
To explore pathways to progression… 65
Or continue to success and luck…

11. Is Success About Being Lucky?

A study conducted in 2019 concluded that 50% of career success is down to luck[1]. And of course, some folk *do* appear to be luckier than others, for example, having it 'handed to them on a silver plate' because they happened to be born into a successful family. Others, on the other hand, may appear to experience greater misfortune in their lives, experiencing tragedy after tragedy. However, how much of this 'success = luck' formula is *reality* and how much of it is *perception*?

Richard Wiseman[ii] carried out research suggesting that, on the whole, luck is about perception... i.e. how we interpret our lot in life. Two people might experience quite similar events and one person will see the positives in it, whilst the other person will focus on the negatives. Indeed, two of the most motivational and influential events in my life was losing a job early in my career and living next to a psychotic neighbour! Losing the job meant focussing full time on developing my own business... no excuses! The experience with the neighbour led us to sell and move to another house... which put us in a good position soon after to buy our 'forever' home. We wouldn't have been motivated to move (psychologically and literally) if we hadn't had such a hellish time; instead, without the neighbour, comfort may have led to complacency and we might still be living there.

But what if luck is not just about *perception*, but also about the *reality* of the action a person takes in preparation. Most 'overnight success stories' have years of hidden effort behind them. As mentioned elsewhere (Piece 9), 'fortune favours the brave'. Those who get proactive and take action are more likely to achieve their outcomes. Of course, you may face challenges of inequality, unfairness and the ineptitude of others... but remember: there is probably someone out there who started with more challenges than you and who still achieved far greater things than you might ever want to achieve. Model these people and get inspired!

Bravery is also about 'getting outside your comfort zone'... sailing into unknown waters... facing the demons, dragons and hobgoblins at the edge of your map (here be monsters!) When you choose to grow, develop and expand your map, the uncertainty of the unknown disappears. Confidence develops as you *trust yourself* more and more to be able to handle whatever life throws at you.

As well as being influenced by proactivity and bravery, fortune will also be enhanced by a degree of talent (i.e. being good at what you do) and by qualities such as passion, perseverance, imagination, intellectual curiosity and openness to experience[iii].

A friend of mine, when told how lucky she is for running such a successful business would reply: "It's funny, the harder I've worked, the luckier I've been!" Of course, it is not all about hard work... but the more focussed, smart, targeted, purposeful effort you put in, the more successful you are likely to be.

How much do you want success... and how dedicated, creative and open are you prepared to be?

To discover why people do (or do not) achieve goals... 22
To be prepared for success... 109
Or continue to the crossroads of luck ...

12. Meet You at the Crossroads!

> *"Luck is at the crossroads,*
> *where opportunity and preparation meet."*

This saying is attributed to many orators[i] and, to some extent, it was the notion of luck, opportunity and preparation that inspired *"**Driving Your Destiny**"*. Everything in this book is about creating and noticing *opportunities* whilst being in a *state of readiness* to take advantage of those opportunities.

In this sense, luck is all about probabilities… So how can we raise our odds, stack the deck and load the dice in our favour? Does this sound like cheating? Let us call it 'ethical cheating'… i.e. getting creative to give yourself the greatest chance of success. (And when it comes to ethics… we'll explore this in Piece 63!)

Can we create more opportunities? Yes, we can… by choosing to go out more and speaking to more people. Will we need to focus and target the opportunities? Yes! It is about being in the right place at the right time. Will we need strategies to tell us that 'this is the right time'? Yes!

Can we increase our level of preparation and readiness? Yes! And this will mean psychological readiness as well as practical. By being in a state of readiness, you are more likely to notice the potential opportunities around you.

I have been told, by others, things like: "You are so lucky to…

- "have a job you enjoy"

- "have a such a wonderful relationship"
- "have a lovely home"
- "have time to write books"
- "have such a well-behaved dog"

Of course, this is someone else's relative perspective and may say more about them than me. However, all of the pathways I have taken have been a choice (often a considered choice) and they took an investment of time, prioritising and purposeful effort. None of them happened by themselves, nor happened immediately nor came to me from no-where. What each of us has in our life is a result of the 'readiness for opportunity'.

In any potentially opportune situation, ask yourself:

- What problems can I solve here?
- What needs can I meet here?

And do some folk, through no fault of their own, lose the very things that they have built or developed? Yes, of course. But the test is how they respond. Successful, resilient people will grieve and feel the pain of loss... and then they refocus, make meaning, learn and get back in the driving seat of their own luck.

To expand on your choices... 45
To explore how networking can build readiness... 101
Or continue to when opportunity knocks...

13. When Opportunity Knocks!

What if more opportunities arise than we think? What if they are there… but we simply don't notice them?

Over time, I have met folk who have expressed an interest in what I do… with a view to getting into the same type of business. And I have told each and every one of them that I would be happy to help in any way I could. However, almost none of them followed up on the conversation. This made me wonder how many times I might have done the same… missed a clear signal and not followed up.

Here are some quick do's and don'ts:

- Do not wait for someone to notice you: this rarely leads to ongoing success. Be prepared to *get* noticed.
- Do not expect someone to spoon-feed you with your career success. Be proactive and get in the driving seat.

The point here is… you never know where a conversation might take you. It may lead to nowhere… but it may open up a new doorway. And be prepared to push the door open. Do not stand and wait for someone else to open it for you. If you need to find or create a 'permission' (e.g. "is it okay if I call you?"), then get permission… and follow up!

If you think you might be (or going to be) in an opportune moment, ask yourself the following:

- What is the potential in this situation?

- Whose 'permission' might I need in order to develop this (e.g. who is the decision maker)?
- What does the other party need?
- How might I be of service or be a benefit to the other party?
- What could I co-create with the other party?

Do not simply wait for opportunities to happen. You need to be proactive and *make* opportunities happen! Remember, it is not just what presents itself at that moment in time, it is where your current situation might lead you. Be prepared to visit places you might not always go. For example, take a walk around your organisation and explore the floors you have not been before...

What opportunities have you created recently? What different places have you been to? What have you gone out and sought? Who have you spoken with to unlock the opportunities?

Interesting things can happen on a pathway... and sometimes they take us sideways into new or eventful adventures.

Remember though, you don't have to take **all** the opportunities in front of you! Be aware of the risk factors (the dark alleys as it were).

Trust your heart with opportunities – follow those that make your heart **sing** and be cautious of those that make your heart sink.

To explore what makes your heart sing... 35
To handle the 'no opportunities trap'... 114
Or continue to a state of readiness...

14. A Perpetual State of Readiness!

"If you were waiting for the opportune moment... that was it!"
Captain Jack Sparrow

In order to grab opportunities fully and effectively, you will need to be ready and prepared for those magic moments as they arise. You will need to be able to recognise the opportune moments and utilise them!

You have (or will soon have) a set of life goals, career aspirations and chosen pathways (each with their own wonderful branches of potential and possibility). For every one of these pathways, what is your 'ASK' (Attitude, Skills, Knowledge)?

In order to take the next steps towards your desired outcome, how will you need to be, what skills do you need to develop and what do you need to know?

- **Attitude**: This includes your 'inner state' and qualities. For example: confidence, motivation, wellbeing, satisfaction, passion, persistence and loving what you do. Attitude is about preparing yourself psychologically. For each quality you need (or would like) to develop, ask yourself: "How would I know I had this quality?" Turn the inner states into behaviours and actions: "What would I do differently if I had that?"

- **Skills:** Your key skills are those abilities that will serve you and make your life easier, for example: presentation, assertiveness, leadership, negotiation, influencing, time management, networking, interviewing. How can you develop yourself (i.e. enhance your capability, productivity and ability to deliver)? Then, what technical/core/stem career skills do you need in order to be able to do a specific job?

- **Knowledge**: Your knowledge is the accumulated useable information you have gathered over time. It is about your ability to sort through data, to understand situations and to demonstrate wisdom in your decisions and actions. This may be technical/specialist knowledge, related to your profession, and knowing what and how to deal with a multitude of scenarios. Knowledge is also about your ability and commitment to learning and *learning how to learn*!

To explore life and career goals… 30
To develop your presentation skills… 53
Or continue to all-ready employed…

15. *All-Ready Employed?*

Perhaps you are already employed... but are you *all-ready* employed? Are you prepared for the next step in your journey?

Most people wait until crisis hits and/or they are out of a job to then start getting ready for a new role. This is the point where they begin networking and updating their CV! However, if you are employed now... this is the *best time* to get into a state of readiness:

- keep your CV current,
- keep adding relevant and interesting connections to your professional network,
- keep an eye on what else is out there jobwise and what the market place is doing.

In effect... up-keep to keep up!

If you are looking to become self-employed, do your market research *whilst* you are employed. Put a website together (i.e. an online brochure for your new business) whilst you are still receiving an income. Do what you can to develop interest in your new venture. Network and connect with those involved and/or interested in your new field. Test out the market place to see if there is a need. Is it something you could earn a living doing?

If you are looking to move onwards and upwards, make sure you are succession planning with your team... who could replace you? Develop others and take the risk of making yourself dispensable in your current job! At the same time, seek delegation from your own manager and get involved in other projects that add to your experience and skillset. On top of this, make sure you are psychologically ready to move upwards. In many organisations, the higher you go, the less support you will get… it can become 'lonelier' as you step up and progress.

The same applies if you are looking for any type of career change (including moving location): begin creating a network in the new area before you make that change.

Wherever and whenever you can, use the platform you currently have as a stable base to get prepared for the next level or a new adventure. This will give you both a foundation for your next steps **and** a contingency plan if the unexpected happens.

At all times in your career, even if you love your job and the company you work for, maintain your state of career readiness. This also applies towards the end of your career, getting ready to wind down. Too many people retire and then become depressed because their identity is locked into their job and they don't know what to do with themselves.

No matter where you are on your journey, make sure the next step is going to be meaningful and fulfilling.

To develop a flexible CV… 93
To prepare for the effects of success…108
Or continue to starting a business…

16. Thinking of Starting a Business?

Moving from being employed to self-employed can be a risky venture, particularly if it is your first time. Be prepared for your business to take a year or so to build up (unless you already have an excellent network of folks who have already promised to pay for your services). Hence... make sure you can afford it.

Do as much as you can whilst you are employed to get the business up and running. Although this is not a book specifically geared to the intricacies of setting up a business, here are some questions you will want to consider and address:

- What is your passion and hence your mission?
- What is your purpose? Why are you starting this specific business?
- What is your product/service?
- Who, specifically, are you serving and how?
- What problems will you solve and needs will you meet?
- How will people recognise that they need you and how will they find you?
- How much will you charge?
- How unique is your offering... and what makes it so special?
- Why will people come to you and continue to use you?
- How will you measure and record your success?
- Who else can help you in making this business work?
- Who else will you need (specialists, professionals etc.), where are they and how will you afford them?
- Where will you work (e.g. at home, rent an office/unit)?

When you take the leap, you need to know that you can survive happily whilst you continue to build up the business. Depending on what you new venture is, it could take two years of hard work in marketing and sales to build up enough customers (and hence money to pay the bills).

For some, the transition from working with others to working (e.g. at home) alone can be an isolating experience. So, what networks will *you* plug into?

I don't write all of this to put you off... however, it is essential to be as realistic as you can be about your idea. Most new business owners have to be (initially) a salesperson, marketeer, planner, proposal writer, designer, service provider, producer, deliverer, accountant, IT specialist... you get the idea!

Write a business case, explore the risks and figure out the mitigations to the risks. For each thing that could go wrong along the way, you will want a range of solutions in place to prevent or cure those challenges.

I have met too many folks over the years who have left a job to start a new business, only to find that they were not ready for the reality. So, if you are currently employed, use this time to plan and set up the new business before you leave. You might also consider a staged approach... for example, can you reduce your hours or go part time?

To explore the purpose of being...32
To make networking easier... 102
Or continue to your career focus...

17. Where is Your Career Focus?

Here, we introduce the PROMPT model (which can help you to determine your current career focus). Where are you now?

Problem Focus ➡ **Remedy Focus** ➡ **Outcome Focus** ➡ **Model Focus** ➡ **Process Focus** ➡ **Test Focus**

Problem Focus…

With problem focus, a person tends to feel a victim to life/the system/their organisation. They act as if at they are at the mercy of their current situation. They may talk about how awful their current job is and how terrible their managers are. They will often appear quite 'down' or depressed about their lot in life and forget the good things they do have. They use phrases like: "the problem is…" or "the trouble with this place/my job is…". If you offer them suggestions, they may reply: "the difficulty with that would be…".

What is it that I do not *want anymore?*

Remedy Focus

With remedy focus[i], the person realises that they are not happy with where they are and what is happening around them. They start saying: "I do not like this. I do not want this. This is not satisfying me anymore. This is not okay. I do not want to be here. There must be more to life than this." They have reached a level of dissatisfaction but have at least understood and acknowledged it. They have progressed from Problem State but are still unable to figure out what they want.

When I'm not 'here' (problem state), where will I be?
What is it that I want instead?

Outcome Focus:
With outcome focus, you realise what it is that you *do* want. You have a goal, a direction, a 'due north'. This is the point where you get in the driving seat, make some decisions and choose your destination. Here, you might say: "This is what I want in my life and my career..."

Who else has got to where I want to be?
How did they achieve that?

Model Focus:
With model focus, you begin to identify who else has achieved what you want to achieve. You then look at how they have achieved it and what you could learn from that.

How could I get from here to where I want to be?
What are some of my options?

Process Focus:
In process focus, you know what you want and you have plans in place to make it happen. You know where you want to get to and you have a route mapped out. You also have a sense of things that could get in the way... and how you might overcome them. You plan for the worst but hope for the best!

Test Focus
In test focus, you are taking action. You are being proactive... getting out there... doing and reviewing as you go!

To explore what outcomes & goals give you... 21
To discover what makes your heart sing... 35
Or continue to coach yourself...

18. Be Your Own Career Coach!

You may have realised that it is possible to be your own coach, both in terms of goal setting and problem solving. Of course, sometimes it can be useful to get external help from someone (e.g. an executive coach, mentor or training event) who can provide another perspective, ask you new and different questions, answer your questions and help you to stay accountable.

To return to the PROMPT model (introduced in Piece 17), here are some useful questions you can use to move yourself from stuck-ness to solution:

Problem Focus

- What is the situation/problem? What are the likely causes/root causes?
- What if anything, has stopped you achieving your goal/solving your problem already? (Do you need to overcome these barriers before proceeding?)

Remedy Focus

- What are the consequences of not solving this problem (or the situation remaining as it is)?
- What are the potential benefits of solving the problem (or improving the situation)?
- What is your motivation level (Scale 1-10) – i.e. how big an issue is it and/or how much do you want things to change?

Outcome Focus

- What do you need?
- What specifically do you want to achieve?
- How will you know you have achieved it?

- How will others know you have achieved it?
- What resources might you need and how does this differ to what you have?
- When do you want to have achieved this by?

Model Focus

- Who is already good at this or has solved/achieved this already? How would they approach it?
- What resources do you have available, e.g. people, knowledge, skills?
- What would you get by solving the problem/achieving your goal? How might you gain those things in other ways?

Process Focus

- What options do you have? What could you do?
- Which option will you take and what is your process/plan?
- What (if any) negative consequences, risks or barriers could arise from taking this option? How will you handle each of these?
- What are the steps you will take (including time-lines)?
- How can you keep yourself motivated? Who could help?

Test Focus

- What action are you taking now?
- How is it going? What are you learning? What is going well?
- What might you change/do differently to help you get to where you want to be?

To understand your belief bubble… 37
To overcome the issue of 'not enough time'… 110
Or continue to circles of influence…

19. Circles of Influence

Those folks who are happier and more resilient tend to focus on what they *can* do something about. They seek to understand what they can control and what they can influence.

Control usually implies something we can change under our own volition. Influence may require the help and support of others.

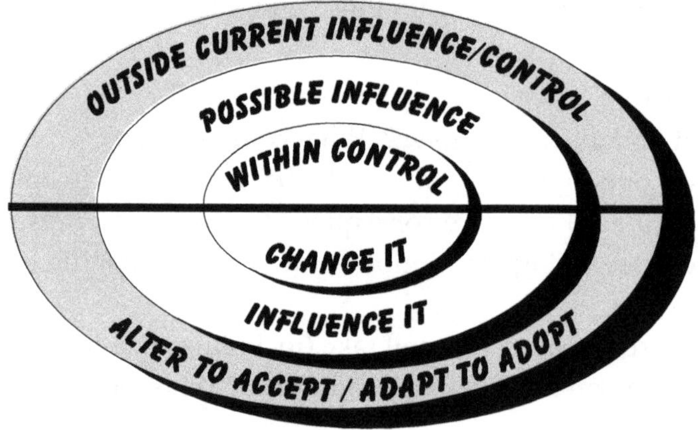

Do not let external factors and pressures become an excuse for inaction (e.g. "the end result is outside of my control, so why bother!") Some goals (and problems) need to be broken down into parts, particularly if they are large or complex. You may find that some elements will be within your control whilst others may not.

Which parts can I do something about,
which parts require help from others and
which parts are outside my current control and influence?

Things outside your control and influence could be labelled:

'This is the way the world/organisation (etc) is'.

Or, more simply:

'It is what it is!'

If you expect things to be different or think they *should* be different than they actually are... then this will put you in the passenger seat... and add to the stress. When we think people or things 'should' be a particular way (and they are not), this is known as the *'fantasy-reality gap'*. It is important to close this gap, either through acceptance or by stepping up and taking action to make change happen.

To deal with pressure... 111
To bring certainty to uncertainty... 122
Or continue to out of control: into control...

20. Out of Control: Into Control

Sometimes we are faced with problems and barriers that we can apparently do nothing about.

Approach 1: Who do I know that has the power to solve that problem or remove that barrier? How might I influence them to help me?

Approach 2: Understand that a problem is only a problem to you personally *if it actually impacts* on you in some way[i]. There are plenty of problems 'out there' that are not your problems.

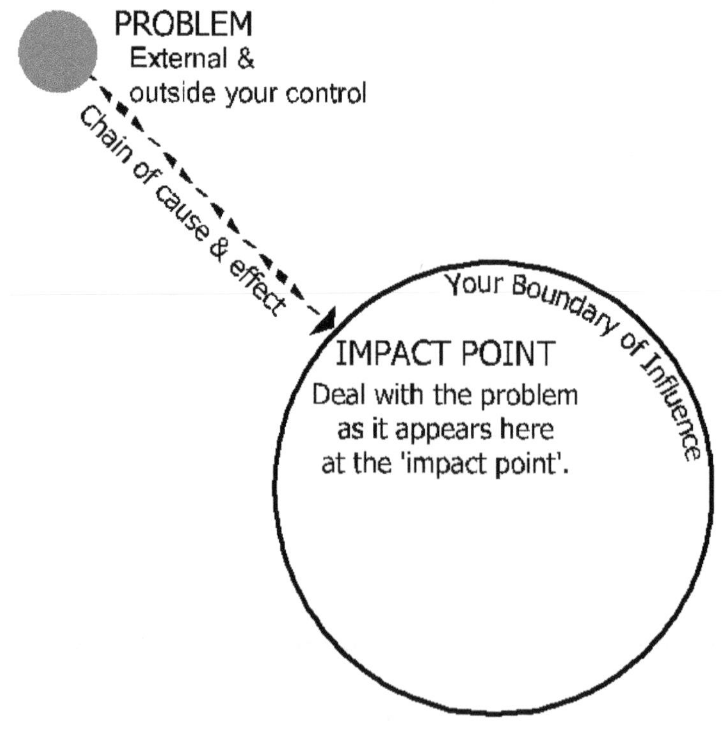

If something is genuinely outside your influence/control then you need to look at your 'interface' with the problem (i.e. the 'Impact Point') and deal with it there.

Ask yourself:

How does that affect me directly?

You will find the answer(s) to this question will usually be about '*resources*' (e.g. it impacts on my time or finances) or '*feelings*' (e.g. it makes me feel angry, upset, anxious). Then, to move forward, get creative about ways to manage your resources (e.g. time, money) and/or develop some strategies for handling your emotions. Ask yourself: "How do I want to feel differently about this?" Then: "How might I do that?"

Approach 3: What group might be able to influence the situation (and can I join that group)? For example, via petitions or by getting the team together to influence the situation. One person alone may not be able to solve the problem, but a group in consensus may create more leverage.

Approach 4: Consider what opportunities this 'crisis' might present to you… and how might you capitalise on those opportunities?

To get in the driving seat of your own brain state… 41
To learn how to dissolve dilemmas… 107
Or continue to understanding why goals are not gaols…

21. Goals are not Gaols!

Why do some people resist having goals?

Some people seem to find goals restrictive, as if they are losing some sense of freedom by setting a goal to get to a specific destination. However, goals do not have to be gaols (i.e. jails)!

There may be challenges on route of course. The word 'goal' is an old English word that links to barriers and hinderances. Then, over time, it became a word linked to a way or a course. Even today, both of these may be true. Achieving goals often requires handling obstacles on our journey from where we are now to our desired destination.

Another distinction we could make is between goals, aims and objectives. Aims give us a direction but are looser and more general wish-oriented outcomes. Objectives are more formal and formulaic. Most folks in the business world have encountered SMART objectives, which is a set of criteria for making sure your outcomes are specific, measurable, achievable/agreed, realistic/relevant and timebound. However, whilst logical, SMART does not address motivation, will or desire.

A goal without motivation is an objective!

What do goals give you?

A meaningful goal will not only be measurable in some way (so you know how you are getting on), but also provides *directionality* and *motivation*. A meaningful goal can become your Magnetic North on the compass of life!

And what if you set a goal… but later don't want it or get bored with it? Then change it! Do not let a goal become a chore. Do it because you are determined and delighted to do it. A career goal needs to excite you. And it is okay if the goal you set is similar to what you already have (and are doing) now… but with more bells and whistles!

In order to have a goal, *you don't have to* not *like* where you are now (and the double negative is intentional there)! You can find happiness/satisfaction with where you are now *and* plan/act towards your destination. Rather than focusing on 'what I don't like about where I am now', consider what you *enjoy* and *gain* from what you do now… and make sure you keep these things going forward. Having said that, if the only way you can 'make' yourself take action is to remember that where you are now is not where you want to be… that is fine too: use the 'away from' motivation as well as the 'towards' motivation if you need it.

To explore the destination in the journey… 26
To understand your role in your destiny… 115
Or continue to those that achieve goals…

22. Those That Achieve Goals & Those That Do not

Have you ever been curious about those people who seem to be able to focus on and achieve what they want in life?

The question is: how do *you* create life and career goals that are compelling, meaningful *and* keep you in the driving seat (even in the face of roadblocks and obstacles)?

Fortunately, there is a model for setting goals so that they are more likely to get achieved. This model is a set of criteria that comes from neuro-linguistic programming (NLP) and is known as 'well formed' outcomes[i]. We have our own version of the criteria, with the acronym: POISED! Like when you are totally ready… on the edge of your seat…

Positive — Needs to be positively stated. Focus on what you **do** want.

- *What do you want/need?*

Owned — Needs to be about you and not about someone else. You are responsible for your goal!

- *Which part of your goal is about you/within your control?*

Intentional — Needs to identify what you *really* want and perhaps why you want it (i.e. the benefits to you).

- *What would you get by achieving that?*

Sensorial — Needs to be measurable in terms of the senses (see, hear, feel).

- *How will you know you've achieved it? (What will you see, hear, feel?)*

Ecological Needs to work positively for you and your environment (including family and health).

- *What might happen if you went ahead with your goal (positive and negative consequences)?*

Determined Needs to be purposeful and on your timeline (has a timeframe and an end point).

- *By when do you want to have achieved this and how much time will you give it?*

You may already be familiar with SMART objectives[ii]:

- Specific
- Measurable
- Achievable/Agreed
- Realistic/relevant
- Time bound

SMART is good for gauging the 'external' and 'logical' aspects of a goal. POISED explores the 'internal' and 'psychological' factors that are important to you and your environment (e.g. motivation).

If you want to go 'belt and braces', then use both criteria!

To discover what to do if goals seem out of reach… 24
To explore life goals… 30
Or continue to the language of goal motivation…

23. *The Language of Goal Motivation*

What do you say to yourself when you have a goal in mind?

Some phrases we use don't give us enough 'oomph' to tip us into taking action or making things happen. Other phrases can give us the internal boost we need.

Think of something that you are mildly interested in having or making happen. What do you say to yourself about this goal? Then think of something you are hugely passionate about... where nothing can stop you! What do you say to yourself about this goal?

Think of a goal you have now and then run through the following phrases, adding your goal to the end of the phrase. Notice the difference each of these statements has on you psychologically and physiologically:

- ❖ I *wish* I could...
- ❖ I'd *like* to...
- ❖ I **could**...
- ❖ I ***want*** to...
- ❖ I ***need*** to...
- ❖ I **have** to...
- ❖ I ***must***...
- ❖ I ***can...***
- ❖ I ***will***...
- ❖ I'm ***going to***...
- ❖ I'm**...** [*add 'ing' to the verb*]
- ❖ I **am**... [*add 'ing' to the verb*]

For example, if 'write a book' is your goal:

- I *wish* I could write a book.
- I'd *like* to write a book.
- I **could** write a book.
- I *want* to write a book.
- I *need* to write a book.
- I **have** to write a book.
- I *must* write a book.
- I *can* write a book.
- I *will* write a book.
- I'm *going to* write a book.
- I'm writing a book.
- I **am** writing a book.

Which of these feel the least and most powerful to you? Which seem wishy-washy and which give you 'oomph'! Now go and oomph it... and enjoy achieving your goal!

To discover more about your values... 34
To explore other ways of managing your state... 43
Or continue to when goals seem out of reach...

24. When Goals Seem Out of Reach

"But the stars we could reach were just starfish on the beach..."
Terry Jacks (Seasons in the Sun)

Some folk don't *realise* their goals because the goals are either unrealistic in terms of potential (e.g. run 100 meters in 6 seconds unaided at the age of 50... *one day it might be possible but not at this time!*) or in terms of resources and time (e.g. to become a millionaire in the next week).

Of course, I am not wanting to place limits on anyone and, so, I like the 'formula' used in the coaching world[i]:

Performance = Potential - Interference

The idea here is that we all have potential and we all have obstacles (i.e. interference). Some people have more obstacles than others and if your goal is highly ambitious (which equates to extreme performance), you may (or may not!) have more barriers to deal with. It is useful therefore to list out the likely obstacles and plan accordingly to remove or work round them.

What if we, ourselves, are the obstacle? What if we get in our own way? How do we know that and what can we do? The first step is to answer this question (i.e. list out the reasons):

What has stopped you from achieving this goal already?

Many of the things you have on your list of reasons will be 'limiting beliefs'. Some of these will be 'world beliefs' about the situation and the way the world works (e.g. "there are already lots of people out there doing what I do"). Some of them will be self-beliefs about your own ability to achieve the goal (e.g. "I'm not good enough at presentations to make a good impression"); this could include self-beliefs about disabilities and 'hidden disabilities' (e.g. dyslexia) that might hold someone back.

Here is the 'driving seat' challenge to barriers and limiting beliefs. It too is a belief… but it can be a massively empowering one:

Someone else out there has started with less and achieved more!

If someone else, at some point in history, has started out with less resources than me but has achieved my goal and more… for me, this removes my excuses… all of them! Either, we need to find someone who has done what we want to do and ask them how they did it. Or we can accept that it is probably true and then simply use it as a motivator to keep going until we get to where we want to be.

Indeed, when you meet folk who faced the odds to get to where they are… they are usually the ones who have learnt the most along the way. Often, these are the folk who have amazing stories of handling adversity! Learn from them, apply the learnings and get inspired!

To discover how modelling can help… 27
To explore your 'belief bubble'… 37
Or continue to add flexibility to tough goals

25. *Adding Flexibility to Tough Goals*

Would you be happy to win £10 million on the lottery? Assuming the answer is 'yes'(!), ask yourself why? How would that help you? What would that give you? How would your life be different (in a good way)?

If you want to learn something about yourself, take time to write a list of things you would get by winning the lottery. When you have written the list, look at each item: if it is a tangible 'thing' (e.g. expensive sports car, mansion etc) then ask the same question again for each of these items (i.e. and what would *that* give me?). For example, a sports car might give you the experience, the prestige, the feeling of speed. Eventually, you will end up with a list of things you have already or could gain access to with a bit of creative thinking.

It is not the thing itself that we desire,
but what it means to us, what it gives us.

This provides you with greater *flexibility* because it encourages you to think about *why* you want to achieve the goal and hence could your 'positive intentions' (motivations) be met another way?

What would I get by achieving that goal?

Write a list... and whatever your answers are to the question above, are there other ways of gaining these things ('positive intentions') with alternative solutions?

I once read an article about a football referee and he was asked what led him to getting (and wanting to get) that job. Apparently, he was in a job he didn't like and was on a course about goal setting. Perhaps to annoy the course trainer, he said he wanted to be a top division football player (at the age of 33 and only ever played 'Sunday Pub League'). He was asked to write down what being a top division player would give him. Football was his passion and he knew the game inside-out. He wanted to play on the famous pitches… with the famous players… in front of the big crowds… to be participating in the game, not just watching it. Being paid to do it was nice, but not the main driver. He was then asked how else he might achieve those things. He came up with the idea of an adjudicator (linesman or referee). He looked into it and trained up as a referee. Some years later, he had made it to the top.

If you have goals in life that seem too difficult, check the positive intentions and seek other ways to meet them.

To explore pathways to progression… 65
To use 'positive intentions' to solve dilemmas… 107
Or continue to the destination in the journey…

26. The Destination is in the Journey!

On the journey, the destination is all that matters…
At the destination, the journey is all that matters…
So, enjoy the journey!

Have you ever heard yourself (or someone else) say: "I'll be happy when…" (e.g. "I've finished this report" or "I have more financial freedom")?

It is as if the happiness relies on the completion or end of something (i.e. the destination). But why not be happy NOW whilst on the journey to your destination! Be happy whilst writing the report or on the road to financial freedom!

For some people, success is about money. Indeed. their *goal* is about money (e.g. to make/earn some-such pounds a year). However, money is not an end in itself… and if it is the sole motivation or destination, it is a very poor and impoverishing experience, both on the journey and at its end.

If money is the sole driver, ask yourself 'why?'. What does the money really give you? What does it allow you to do that you cannot apparently do now? These are the real and *meaningful* things that you are working towards. Make money the by-product of your success, not the success in itself.

Making Goals Meaningful

Think of a goal you have… how will you feel when you have achieved it? What will you see, feel, hear and be at that point? What if you could harness this brilliant feeling state for your journey... to help motivate you in the process of achieving the goal (rather than waiting till the end)?

In order to access the 'right' state for a goal, John Overdurf[i] introduced the concept of 'end-state energy'. You can access your 'end-state' by asking: "how will I feel when I achieve this goal?" Whilst accessing/feeling the 'end-state,' ask: "what is the next smallest step I need to take to achieve the goal?" By repeating this process as necessary, you can use the motivation this provides to take you another easy step towards success.

I use this method to help me write books. It is a step-by-step, word-by-word, page-by-page process. Every time I start, I think... "just a hundred words" and that feels easy enough. Before long, I have written lots more than that... and I am another step further towards completing another book[ii].

To start the journey... 30
To discover more about states... 43
Or continue to do some modelling...

27. *Do Some Modelling!*

You don't have to dress up and strut your stuff on the catwalk to develop your career… unless you are seeking to be a catwalk model. And of course, what you get up to in your spare time is up to you.

The modelling we are exploring here is the process of identifying the strategies of a role-model or exemplar[i]; this could be a person (or thing) that is particularly successful in the area you would like to develop. By modelling them, you can accelerate your learning and give yourself more options in driving your destiny.

The first step is to select a role-model. It could be someone you know personally or someone you don't know but identify with in some way. It could be someone historical or even fictional. Most importantly, it can be *yourself* when you have excelled in the past or when you are in a different context (i.e. somewhere else in life where you are confident and good at what you do).

- Who has got to where I would like to get to?
- Who has achieved what I would like to achieve?
- Who is already good at this?

The second step is to identify how they *approach* the situation (practically and psychologically), and then what they actually *do* (their strategy) in that context (again both practically and psychologically). The strategies someone uses might be about their longer-term plans and successes (e.g. how they have got to where they are in their career) or actions (e.g. how they handle being put on the spot in a meeting).

- How would they approach this? How would they feel? What might they be thinking? How might they prepare?
- What would they do in this situation? How might they respond?
- How have they got to where they are (what steps)?

If you are a new manager who is in a difficult situation, you might ask yourself: "My best ever manager… how would they have dealt with this?"

If you know someone who has what you would like, e.g. a big house, a senior role, their own successful business etc., rather than getting jealous… get curious. They may not have achieved these things instantly. If you can, ask them how they got to where they are. Perhaps it took them twenty years of hard work to get there. Ask them what things they did that *really* made a difference… the best decisions they made. Then, what can you learn from them?

To model calmness and being in the now… 46
To model being 'impeccable'… 63
Or continue to modelling confidence…

28. *Modelling Confidence*

There may be certain areas in life where we would like to be more confident. So, what if we could transfer confidence from someone or somewhere else?

If you want to model someone else's confidence, take a moment to imagine that person. Then, when you get a good sense of them looking confident, step into their shoes. Literally move yourself into copying their posture, how they stand, their facial expression... and move like them. You are not actually being them; you are taking on their persona and behaviours. You are still you... but with a new set of resourceful behaviours that you can play with!

When I very first started presenting, I modelled a confident Australian presenter I knew. I walked like him, carried a handful of flipchart pens like he did. I even had an Australian accent to start with! Within a short period of time, I was happy being me at the front of the room. It was a useful confidence boost to get me started.

Alternatively, rather than using someone else's confidence, you can use your own, or rather, the *confident you,* as a role-model. Here are the key steps:

1) Consider a scenario where you would like to feel (and come across as) more confident, e.g. chairing meetings, participating in senior meetings, presenting, negotiating, interviewing or being interviewed etc.
2) Write down how you would like to be or what you would like to be able to do in that scenario.

3) Then write down your concerns (or what stops you from being confident here).
4) Now think of a scenario where you are totally confident, something you enjoy doing, something you know you are good at. It does not have to be related to the non-confident situation. For example, the thing that you are confident doing might be riding a horse, baking a cake, driving, dancing, cycling, playing a particular sport etc.
5) Take your concerns (from step 3) and imagine them occurring in your confident scenario. You may need to treat this somewhat metaphorically. How would you be and what would you do?

For example, what if someone is quiet in meetings but good at dancing. We would ask: "What if speaking up in a meeting and getting yourself heard (*non-confident*) was like dancing on the dance-floor (*confident*)?" Let's say that their concern was not being able to get a word in to make their point:

Concern/Need	**Confident Context**	**Confident Strategy**	**Apply to problem context**
Getting a word in to make my point. Creating space to express myself.	How would I create a space in which to express myself on the dance-floor?	Move forward, use body language to map out my space and dance anyway.	Sit forward, use a gesture (e.g. put hand on table), then at the smallest gap, talk anyway – speak with a strong voice!

The more you map confidence onto a 'non-confident' situation, the more confident-associated neural connections you add.

To model confidence when put on the spot… 77
To model effective networkers… 103
Or continue to modelling metaphors…

29. Modelling Metaphors in Nature

If you want to generate new ideas and strategies for dealing with a challenge or a barrier, you might try modelling *nature* as a metaphor. Think about it… nature has solved every problem it has faced so far. The natural world is possibly the most resourceful model you could use to generate new thinking.

Think of a challenge or goal you have. Now imagine: what if that challenge or goal was represented as a scenario in nature? For example, if you want to build connections with more senior leaders, how might that translate to the natural world, i.e. how do animals, plants and elements reach important things that are initially out of reach?

Write a list and then use your 'nature' examples as metaphors to spin new ideas for yourself. For example:

- Fly, float or jump up. *Are you prepared to take the leap or create opportunities to 'float' about where senior managers gather?*
- Glide across from another high vantage point. *Which other senior connections could help you?*
- Grow taller. *Could you put yourself forward for projects/presentations?*
- Climb other things that are tall. *Who could refer you to those you want to speak to?*
- Bring the 'out of reach' things down to you. *What role could you take on to cause those people to want to seek you out and talk to you? (E.g. be an expert in something useful or become editor of the company newsletter)*

- Be seen from the ground. Look attractive and interesting! *How might you raise your profile and get seen?*
- Wait by the watering hole. *(AKA coffee area!)*
- Symbiosis. *Who could you help that could also help you?*

I am sure you can come up with many more examples from nature that will then generate even more ideas to address the challenge you are facing.

The beauty of using a metaphor like nature is that you are stepping outside of the limitations of your current 'problem'. This, in turn, can allow you to be more creative in generating ideas. The fun trick is then to map those ideas back to your situation and see what new ideas are generated.

To model interview readiness... 96
To model dealing with change... 120
Or continue to the journey's start...

30. And the Journey Always Starts Here

No matter where you are in your life and your career, there will always be places to go and things to do!

Do you have a 'bucket list'? Planet Earth is an amazing place and this life we have is an extraordinary gift! What dreams do you have… of things you would like to have happen?

In a reflective moment, consider the following questions (at different times, some questions may resonate more than others):

- *What would you like to do?*
- *Where would you like to go?*
- *What would you like to have?*
- *What would you like to make?*
- *What do you want to give?*
- *How would you like to contribute?*

And for the answers to each question, consider:

What would doing/going/having (etc) that give you?

This second set of answers will tell you more about *why* you want what you want and hence what is *really important* to you in achieving your goals.

On your journey, sometimes it is the unexplored sideroads and the unexpected adventures that make the story of your life even more interesting!

Will you be the person who looks back on their life and is glad they took action towards making their existence as extraordinary as possible?

Remember that today… right here, right now… you are at the beginning of the next step of what could be a life full of wonder.

And sometimes it not the big things, but those fleeting moments captured and then set free… the simplest of things… the laughter of your loved one… the feeling in your heart as you watch your child (or puppy) sleeping… the sunset that makes you stop and gaze… the smell of a rose, sweet and indescribable… watching pouring rain through the window, when you are cosy and warm inside… the way food and drink can taste different when you are outside… the earthy feeling after a summer storm… the sensation of gentle sunshine on your skin… getting that final crossword clue that has been eluding you…

To explore how you see the world… 39
To discover things to make you feel good… 42
Or continue to your purpose…

The Second Bit

Pieces About You

31. Start with Your Purpose

Congratulations! You have discovered the Piece that is here to answer the age-old question... "What is the Purpose of Life?" More importantly, what is the purpose of *your* life? Perhaps ***the*** Purpose of Life is simply to choose *your own* purpose of life... and then live it to the best of your ability! And might your purpose change? Perhaps... it depends on how specific you are. If your purpose is to enjoy work, you might choose to change it if and when you want to retire! If it is to bring up wonderful children... then you may want to update that when they leave home!

How do *you* answer this 'ultimate' question...

What is your purpose?

Of course, you can explore this through some other questions:

- Why are you here? In order to what?
- Who are you here for? To do what?

As a teenager, heavily embroiled in the personal development world, I woke up one morning with the following three words in my head:

Love, Learn, Enjoy!

These words have served me as my purpose, my due North. To love what I do and to love those that are around me, to learn from others and from the situation, to enjoy what I do and being with others. If there was ever a situation where these were in conflict, they would play out in that order from 'love' first to 'learn' and then to 'enjoy'. This has also developed a little over time:

- To love and be loved.
- To learn and be learned from (i.e. to share what I learn).
- To enjoy and to be enjoyed (i.e. to cause laughter, smiles and light-heartedness).

An interesting way of establishing the purpose of *your job* is to identify what would happen if your job stopped (and no-one else replaced you doing what you do). Because you are part of a system, there would be a sudden hole... certain things would not get done and this would have a ripple effect that would get bigger and bigger. Flip this around and you get to an understanding that (a) your job is essential and (b) what you are *really* here for in your job role.

So, if you applied that to your life... what would happen if you were not there and no-one else replaced you doing what you do? What would not have been done? What would not exist? What would other people have missed out on?

To explore this further, I would recommend watching 'It's a Wonderful Life' by Frank Capra, starring James Stewart. Keep watching... all the way to the end... and then reflect on the positive difference you have made for others in their lives!

To find (and fine tune) your voice... 54
To explore pathways to progression... 65
Or continue to the purpose of being...

32 ...the Purpose of Being

What would you like to be?
Who would you like to be?

These questions of being... or rather your answers to the questions will help you to determine so much in your life and career. They will provide you with a 'touchstone' for your decisions and actions as you journey through life. They will influence (and be influenced by) your mission and your purpose. They will give you a sense of balance, stability and control. At any given moment you can confidently know and embody:

"I have a true sense of who I am in this environment."

This is the wellspring of strength, integrity and courage.

Of course, we could simply answer the questions "who do I want to be?" with "I want to be myself". That is grand... as long as you really know who 'myself' is.

Given who you would like to be, what maxims or 'golden rules' (or guidelines if you prefer) will help you stay on track and bring you back to your purpose?

Here are some maxim examples for whatever you do in your life and career:

- Do the maximum good and least harm for others and for yourself.
- Act from acceptance... not fear.

- To be unconditional is to accept another person for who they are without trying to change them. Acceptance is not just 'tolerance' but receptiveness as if receiving a gift.
- Every problem has a gift for you in its hands.[i]
- Speak your truth with kindness.
- Empathy dissolves anger.
- Embrace your emotions, but do not *impose* them onto others.
- Remember that your truths are simply your beliefs and values. Others will have their own truths. Even if there is an objective Truth, it is not ours to hold.
- The road to enlightenment is not one path in many… it is many paths in one.

Find the words that are meaningful for you… and take time to create your own.

To understand the 'assertive you'… 52
To develop your legacy… 74
Or continue to your story…

33. *And What is Your Story?*

People have stories that define who they are. For some, these stories are 'victim' stories of what has happened to them. For others, it is about things they are proud of. For others, it may be stories of what makes them laugh about life.

It is probable that our identity affects the stories we tell… and then, if we repeat them often enough, the stories will become ingrained into our personality. So, what stories do you tell yourself (and *about* yourself)? Are they potentially destructive or constructive? How about *choosing* the story that you tell in a given situation? Develop flexibility in the types of anecdotes you share… sometimes vulnerable and revealing, sometimes credibility building, sometimes humorous etc.

Another aspect of stories and metaphors is to look outside ourselves, for example at fictional characters and tales. These are known as archetypes… and the archetypes you associate with will determine how you perceive yourself.

As an exercise, consider a book, film, mythological legend, TV show, childhood tale or comic book that you enjoy… something that you resonate with and that sticks in your mind.

If you were a character in that story, who would you be? And, if different, who would you really *like* to be? Perhaps there are a couple of characters you associate with?

If you explore a number of stories, you might end up with a list of characters that appeal to you.

For any character you resonate with, answer the following questions:

- What strengths would that give me?
- What weaknesses might I need to be aware of?
- What permissions would this give me (i.e. what would it allow me to do)?
- What limitations might that bring (i.e. what might that perhaps stop me from doing)?

As well as characters, we can also apply these questions to 'nick-names' we have been given… and to other labels and roles we may have taken on (e.g. I'm the funny one, I'm the clever one).

Examples of characters from *my* personal and professional mythology are: the knight in shining armour, Tigger, Joe Cool (a Snoopy persona), Elrond (from Lord of the Rings) and Doctor Who! Make of that lot what you will!

To enhance your 'brand awareness'… 71
To check your own life patterns… 115
Or continue to understand your values…

34. Understand Your Values

Simply put, your values are those *things that are important to you*. Not the car and house (which are known as 'criteria'), but the intangible things… for example:

Love, excitement, comfort, variety, exploration, politeness, structure, predictability, safety, security, being relaxed, calmness, fun, enjoyment, speed, quickness, being up to date, status, being professional, organisation, control, independence, freedom, autonomy, balance, directness, getting to the point, results, achievement, productivity, delivering, accuracy, looking good, getting good value e.g. for money, fairness, equality, equity, honesty, genuineness, truth, integrity, sharing, open communication, keeping in touch, being kept informed, involvement, kindness, respect, wisdom, clear-thinking, cleverness, intelligence, creativity…

Whilst we may have some core values that are true for every aspect of life, values are generally context specific. For example, think about your answers to:

- What is important to you about relationships?
- What is important to you about work/career?
- What is important to you about home?
- What is important to you about family?

Your values may also change over time, as different things become important and priorities change[i]. Even though they may shift over time or in different contexts, our values are one of the cornerstones of our personality. They may also be considered a 'template' for what we need in life, in work and from others on a day to day basis.

By understanding your values, you will find it easier to be congruent and integrous when making decisions and taking action. It is when we clash with our own values that we feel guilty and demoralised. In addition, we can understand why the behaviour of others sometimes make us angry, resentful and bitter. When someone does something that clashes with our values, we have an emotional reaction. We often want to get angry with them and blame them… "how dare they!"

Consider for a moment the things that others do (or do not do) that irritate you. For example, not thanking you when you open a door for them… what is it that they are not being? Polite? If that is it, you know that 'politeness' is one of your values. From now on, instead of getting angry with other people, you might ask yourself: "Hmm, I wonder which of my values is being clashed there?" (Of course, you might choose not to do that… but it *can* be another great way of establishing your values!)

To discover someone else's values …59
To demonstrate organisational values… 83
Or continue to what makes your heart sing…

35. *What Makes Your Heart Sing?*

You will find that some tasks, activities and projects will give you a buzz. You feel excited and motivated by them. These are the things that make your heart 'sing'!

When someone asks you if you would get involved in something, or do something for them, you might find that your heart sings… or perhaps 'sinks'. Trust this reaction. By all means, ask questions about the commitment to double-check your initial assessment. However, if you have a choice, beware of taking on things that make your heart 'sink'. For example, those things that might give you the 'Sunday afternoon blues': "Oh hell, I've got to go to work tomorrow!"

I have found that by saying a polite 'no' to things that make me 'sink' inside (no matter how financially lucrative they might appear), something else better tends to replace it. And when we ignore the heart… we tend to regret it. Melody (my wife) and I agreed early on in our relationship to trust this reaction and to respect one another in not feeling we have to say 'yes' when we do not really want to.

Why might we get the heart-sink reaction? One explanation is that on some level, we understand that this invitation will not serve us. It will not fulfil us or our values. When you understand your purpose, your mission and your values, you can make decisions that feel aligned to who you are.

When you carry out work that sits well with your values, you will often enjoy it more and feel more passionate about it. If you do a job that fulfils your values… it does not feel like work!

Of course, a particular job or profession may be perfect for you, but the culture, leadership, management or colleagues within a particular organisation may still clash. Here, you have a choice to stay or to leave… but if you do choose to leave, seek a new position that fulfils you… in a company that shares your values. If a company embodies and truly walks the talk of their values, those that stay in the company tend to be those that are in alignment. To put it another other way, people do not tend to stay in companies that have a different value set. It is uncomfortable and unrewarding to have to disagree and rebel all the time!

Realise your passion and make it your profession. Get paid to do what you love!

To make 'heart-sing' choices… 45
To discover other approaches to handling pressure… 111
Or continue to finding good company…

36. Finding Good Company

Why not choose a company to work for that makes your heart sing? There are different types of organisations out there with different drivers. No matter what a company says about itself, you need to dig deeper to establish if it is a best fit for you.

What is the primary driver of the company[i]?

Results Focus	**Stakeholder Oriented** • In business to make money/ reduce cost. • Delivering to shareholders/ owners for financial returns. • *E.g. financial institutions, some retail companies.*	**Cause Oriented** • In business to achieve an outcome. • Driven by 'what is right' or 'needs saving' or 'helping a group'. • *E.g. charities, ethical lawyers.*
Relationship Focus	**Staff Oriented** • In business to enhance welfare, wellbeing and development. • Staff engagement and social responsibility • *E.g. co-operatives.*	**Customer Oriented** • In business to serve, delight and keep the customer happy and loyal. • Based on brand and reputation. • *E.g. restaurants, hospitality.*
	'Internal' Priority'	**'External' Priority**

Each driver orientation has pros and cons, and of course, every organisation has more than one driver… but in what order? Is the customer always right? Will the organisation back a member of staff above a customer complaint? Are staff considered a cost to the business? Is the cause greater than the people? Are the staff treated as individuals or as part of the system? Do some colleagues act aggressively and then say: "Nothing personal, it was just business!" Is it more of a 'company' (of companions) or a 'machine' (of systems and output)?

You can check out the values and culture of an organisation by doing any of the following:

- the company's own website (which is *'what they want the world to see'*)
- websites that review what it is really like to work there
- media news and documentaries (i.e. do they have a good or poor reputation?)
- staff action (e.g. strikes, staff turnover levels)
- what are the business leaders and chief executive like? How are they regarded?

Are you looking for a balance of all four? Or does one area appeal more? Different industries and types of organisations will appeal to different people. Some environments may be more pragmatic than others, some more dynamic; some will be caring and some will fulfil you. Any of them can be a 'great place to work' and any of them can be toxic... and that is usually a reflection of the leadership and/or stakeholders.

Some prefer to work for big organisations (perhaps with more promotional opportunities) and some prefer smaller organisations (where they feel they can make more of a difference). There is no 'perfect' organisation: each will have its own advantages and faults.

Choose wisely!

To be the ethical you... 63
To explore your organisational intelligence... 81
Or continue to understand your belief bubble...

37. Understand Your Belief Bubble

Your belief bubble is one of the cornerstones of your psychological identity. It will drive your unconscious bias, your reactions and your behaviours. It contains your personal judgements and preconceived ideas, for example:

- What is true for you about the world (which as a default position, we assume is The Truth),
- What is true about yourself (this could be limiting or empowering beliefs),
- The way the things are (including the state of the company we work for, the marketplace, management, types/classes/categories of people),
- The way things *should* be (our expectations, the 'rules' of what is okay and not okay, how things should be done – this links with our values).

Our belief bubble might also be described as our 'map of the world'. When we encounter something that does not fit our map, we assume our map is true and that the thing we encountered is wrong or faulty in some way[i]. In addition, if we are given feedback that does not fit our self-beliefs or someone disagrees with our map, we tend to get defensive.

The surface of our bubble has a set of in-built filters that affect the way we process information. In essence, the filters are self-fulfilling… we see what we expect to see. The thicker the wall of the bubble, the more stuck someone is likely to be in their own 'truth' and less accepting of others' truths.

The bubble wall filters out information that does not fit the bubble's content… but if anything breaks through, the bubble wall will also distort information so that it does seem to fit[ii]. In essence, we either 'reject' the new information or we change it to fit what already exists!

This will also be true of self-beliefs. If we have an empowering belief and we hit a setback, we change course and carry on with confidence. If we have a limiting belief, we behave in a less confident fashion and give up more easily, hence confirming our original limiting self-belief. ("See I told you I couldn't do it!")

What is even stranger… if we have a limiting belief but we are successful or get praise/compliments from others, we reject the positive feedback and even put the success down to it being a fluke or one-off. We defend our limiting beliefs as hard as we defend other beliefs!

One way to shift our limiting beliefs (and be more open to other perspectives) is to ask 'reframing' questions:

- How else could I see or interpret that?
- What could I learn from that other perspective?
- What is the other person seeing that I have previously missed?
- What would happen if I said 'thankyou' to praise… and acknowledged that there are people out there that like what I do?

To understand yourself through feedback… 50
To explore the A-B-C of progression… 66
Or continue to understand your bias…

38. Understand Your Bias

Bias, from a psychological perspective, has a number of forms:

- *Unconscious/implicit*: linked to our values and beliefs.
- *Tacit:* what we learn about ourselves and bring to the surface.
- *Purposeful:* our chosen behaviours and spoken/written opinions.

We are all biased... about ourselves, other individuals and groups/types. In order to get a sense of 'self' and identity, we need to know who we are *not* as well as who we are; i.e. there is a me/us and a them (*not* me/us). We then make judgements about 'them' (e.g. different gender, race, age, class, nationality, hair colour, what they wear, who they support, political persuasion, their job role, the company they work for etc.) As uncomfortable as it may be, to be human is to be bias.

However, we **can** recognise our bias and take action to prevent or reduce it. We can choose to change. Indeed, you might treat it as a personal development journey. To be truly non-biased would mean valuing **all** human beings **equally** in whoever they are or whatever they do. It would mean treating them with equal fairness, kindness and equity.

Once you have identified that you may have a bias[i] (or two!), here are some things you might do (in no particular order):

- Choose to step back from first impressions. Remind yourself to look for counter-evidence to your initial assessment of someone.

- If interviewing others, make sure you have some objective measures/criteria for candidates[ii].
- Are you being equal? Ask yourself: Would I treat someone else the same? E.g. if you call a woman 'love', would you call a man 'love' too?
- Visualise/remember someone you like from a similar background to the person you are dealing with now (e.g. race/religion etc.)
- Remember that DIVERSITY IS GOOD! We cannot exist or thrive without diversity (no matter if it creates apparent differences). Differences are not inherently bad, though the mismanagement (personal or organisational) can be destructive.
- Let go of having to be right or that one type is good and the other bad! Seek the possibilities between the absolutes.
- Learn to handle differences more effectively (i.e. seek to understand more about the other party and what motivates them).
- Remember: Empathy dissolves anger. Put yourself in the other person's shoes for a moment. What might they be afraid of? What might they need from *you*?
- Remember: 'Intuition' is simply feedback (usually that which we cannot explain or point to). It can be hard to distinguish between intuition and prejudice. It is not 'fact', so don't treat it as such!
- Read about unconscious bias and the associated language. Educate yourself.

To deal with self-bias... 78
To be on your best interview behaviour... 100
Or continue to how you see the world...

39. How Do You See the World?

When two people look at the state of the world, they might have quite different perspectives and interpretations. One person might speak of the terrible things that are happening, the other might see the positive and the hopeful. These are both perceptions… and the reality is that both perspectives may be 'right' in the sense that we can find evidence for either.

Indeed, there is a whole spectrum of perspectives, ranging from "it's absolutely awful" to "it's extraordinarily wonderful". And wherever we choose to focus (and it *is* a choice), we will find evidence for that!

What you focus on will determine what you'll see.
What you see will determine what you will experience.
What you experience will determine how you feel.

We could argue that ultimately, what you focus on is eventually what you will become. For example, someone who continually focusses on the negative side will eventually become depressed and cynical.

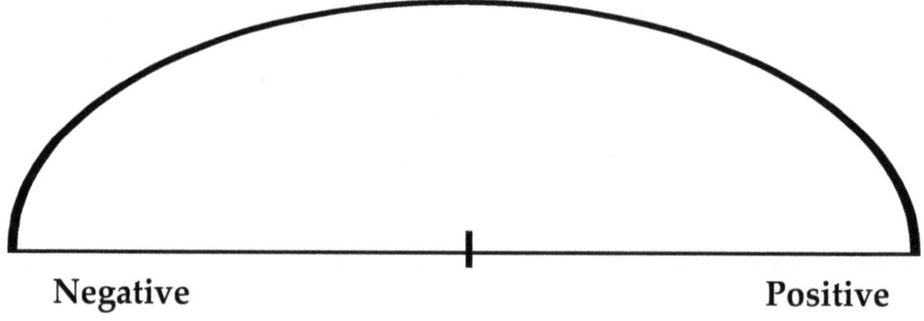

I call this the 'Windscreen of Experience' because depending on where we look through it, it will affect how we filter and hence experience the world. You can apply this model to the world out there, your job, your company, your career… and you can apply this to how you see yourself. For example, if you video yourself doing a presentation… what do you focus on? The bits you like, don't like, or a balance of both? The lesson here is to *change what you don't like but focus on what you* do *like and what* does *work*).

Wherever you are applying the Windscreen, focus on the positive side… **and** be aware of the negative… to change and influence what you can control… but ultimately accept what you cannot change… *It is what it is.* This is *not* about denying the 'negative'… because we cannot act on what we deny.

Here are three things you can do to help yourself:

1. Write down one thing every day that brought you happiness. "The best things that happened today is…" Keep a journal and add to it.
2. Write a list of things you enjoy in your work, life, relationship etc. What do you like… what gives you a buzz?
3. Accept that other people may see the world differently (and have their own evidence to back it up)[i].

It is easier to be enthusiastic about things we like and enjoy... because it helps us to focus on the positive side of the windscreen… and hence affects our wellbeing, resilience and mental health.

To focus on the positive side of yourself… 70
To be the positive force for change... 87
Or continue to resilience…

40. Resilience is Fundamental...

You might never get 'knocked down' by life... but be prepared for it anyway. The more you put yourself 'on the line' and 'out there', the higher the likelihood of rejection and criticism. Indeed, if you don't experience either of these then you are either doing things perfectly... or you may not be doing them right at all!

No matter how fantastic you might be, there will be plenty of folk that do not know or understand that. They may not know they need you. They may not see your potential... or the potential to their organisation in having you on board.

Many (if not most) successful people have been criticised and rejected on their journey. There are websites dedicated to famous authors and the publishers who rejected them and criticised their work[i].

At some point you may experience an active 'no'/'go away' or a passive no reply/no response. So how do you deal with that?

What are some responses to rejection?

- *Passenger seat version*: This person will focus on the hurt and pain, because their identity is shaken and their ego is affronted. They avoid feeling their fear through avoidance, grumbling and playing it safe.
- *Driving seat version*: This person stays philosophical. Instead of: 'taking action means rejection', they see it as: 'rejection means I'm taking action'! They understand that it is a numbers game... the more tickets you buy, the

> more likely you are to win... the more people you talk to and companies you approach... the luckier you will be!

At the very least, learn from rejection. Ask yourself: 'what could I do differently next time?' That does not always mean changing your approach... it may instead mean changing your audience. If you do change your approach, are you pushing or pulling too hard. What would happen if you relaxed and enjoyed the process?

And if you feel like you are getting worn down? Be honest with yourself and then re-motivate: 'Yes, it's difficult/tough/scary... now *come on, let's do it*!'

The most proactive approach, of course, is to *greet* rejection. Learn to love rejection because it means you are participating in the flow of life. You are living and getting 'out there'.

To assess your confidence... 75
To see yourself through another's eyes... 80
Or continue to retrain your brain...

41. Retrain Your Brain (When Under Strain)

Are you in the driving seat of your own brain? If you do not control your brain... who does?

There are, of course, healthy ways to engage your brain and unhealthy ways. The focus here is not to create a hedonistic headrush that lasts forever but rather an ability to change or lift your state when you need to. The brain cannot maintain a chemical state for very long. Indeed, if we try to fixate on high energy states, the brain needs bigger and bigger stimuli to keep it going. This is called addiction… which is certainly *not* being in the driving seat.

All brain chemicals serve a purpose, but they can be destructive if experienced for too long. The brain likes a tidy mind and so likes to clear up after a chemical surge. If we are anxious or feel under constant threat, the brain does not get time to rebalance.

Stress and anger serve a purpose. The 'stress' chemicals, adrenaline and noradrenaline act together, alerting the amygdala (alarm centre) and stimulating the 'fight-flight-fright' response. The system wakes up, the brain and body are motivated to take action. We experience the 'nervous' or excited physiology: heart racing, fluttery sensations as blood rushes to the major muscles, leaving the stomach in butterfly mode. We get a burst of energy and strength…

Perfect for when we need it, this is the sympathetic nervous system in action. However, it does not seem very sympathetic to our system when we are trying to sleep the night before a presentation!

Enter, stage left, the *para*sympathetic nervous system, the balancer, bringing homeostasis to our brain and body chemicals… bringing calm, rest and relaxation. Give yourself a break and let this soothing system do its work.

Alternatively, give your body time and space to recuperate by choosing to partake in relaxing activities:

- Systematic relaxation: Sit or lie quietly, tensing and then *letting go* of each part of your body from toes upwards.
- Meditation: Notice your breathing slowly in… and out. Follow your breathing… and if you notice you are distracted… return to observing your breathing.
- Change your thinking: Choose to see things from another perspective… indeed multiple perspectives… how many perspectives can you see?
- Interrupt internal dialogue: If you realise that your thinking has become destructive in some way (for example, catastrophising about what could go wrong or getting angry with someone in your mind) choose to see those thoughts as silly… tell someone else and have a laugh about it.
- Go for a walk in nature… and see the world as it was meant to be! Relax your gaze and soften your focus… go wide angle with your vision and notice how much more you can see all at once.

To explore how to feel wonderfully unwonderful…44
To handle your inner worrier… 48
Or continue to give your brain a dose of happy…

42. Give Your Brain a Dose of Happy!

There are four 'happiness' chemicals in your brain:

Dopamine *Motivation.*
Oxytocin *Trust and empathy, love, connectedness, bonding.*
Serotonin *Serenity and hopefulness. Good mood.*
Endorphin *Euphoria and determination.*

Dopamine	Oxytocin
• Learn something new. Make a connection. • Create space for 'Aha!' moments, for example, by doing cryptic crosswords. • Achieve a goal or taking a step towards it. Anticipation. Getting a reward of some kind. • Perform acts of kindness to others. • Volunteer and contribute. • Take action, no matter how small. • Celebrate – like your team just scored a goal. "Yes"! • Do the crazy dance! • Get good sleep. • Exercise. • If things seem tough, say to yourself: "Yes, things are tough... *now let's go/let's do this!*" • Jump up and down and make a noise like a gorilla (but not on public transport).	• Socialise with those you like and trust. Be trustworthy. • Build rapport and companionship. • Go back to a networking event and connect with folks you recognise. • Tell people you are happy to be with them and that you are glad you met them. • Show empathy and closeness. • Hug when appropriate and shake hands at networking events! • Listen actively to someone. • Eat with others. • Listen to music and sing. • Praise, compliment and encourage. • Choose only to engage positively with others (including online as well). • Imagine a cuddle with your loved one (if they are not with you) or your pet. • Make eye contact.

Serotonin	Endorphin
• Find meaning, purpose, significance. • Learn to frame and reframe. • Appreciate others. • Do some positive reminiscence/nostalgia. • Remember you are important… you matter. • Show gratitude. Count your blessings. • Enjoy sunshine and bright light. • Notice how you have influenced others and the positive difference you made in their life. • Choose to 'surrender' and let go for a while! • Be in the now. Bring yourself back to the Zero Point (*see 46*). • Acknowledge and accept those things you cannot control.	• Laugh. • Smile. • Have fun and enjoy yourself. • See life through a humour lens… like a cartoon. • Cry at a moving moment or a momentary movie. • Exercise for a better mood. • Stretch. • Do yoga. • Meditate. • Do 'random acts of kindness' for others. • Have a comfortably hot bath[i]. • Go for a walk round the office (or greenspaces). • Watch some silly stuff – videos that raise your spirits. • Do some deeeeep breathing!

Many of the 50 activities listed above (e.g. meditation, exercise and doing random acts of kindness) will promote more than one of the chemicals…

To access your confidence… 76
To work better at home… 112
Or continue to the positive states sheet…

43. Positive States Sheet

What would you like to feel more of… more often?

EXCITED BRILLIANT JOYFUL
CONFIDENT
PASSIONATE PROUD
ENTHUSIASTIC BLISSFUL SUCCESSFUL

EXCELLENT RESILIENT EMPOWERED
RESOURCEFUL COURAGEOUS FUN

OPTIMISTIC HAPPY AMBITIOUS

GRATITUDE CREATIVE FULFILLED

LOVED ADVENTUROUS IN CONTROL
GROUNDED CONNECTED HOPEFUL
CURIOUS INSPIRED IN THE NOW

AUTHENTIC COMPASSIONATE PATIENT
CONTENTED
CALM SINCERITY WISE

The idea of the 'Positive States Sheet' is to use it as a resource for yourself. How often do you see so many positive words all in one place?

Feel free to use this chart… or better still, create your own. Your own words will be so much more powerful because they will be more meaningful to *you*… lighting up your neural network!

If and whenever you want to feel good, start by choosing your state. You have to 'name it to claim it' so how do you want to feel?

Take '*confident,*' as an example. You know what confidence feels like. You have felt confidence in many situations and on many occasions. There will be certain things you do where you are already totally confident. Write a list. And how do you experience confidence? Does it start in your feet and come up? Does it begin with your heart region and spread out? Is it there in your head… in your mind… in your smile as it then waves across the rest of your body? And what body language and posture do you have being confident? How do you move? And what do you say to yourself… "Bring it on!"… "Do it!"… "Come on!"?

Whatever the state you want… it is there inside you already.

To achieve the 'Now' state… 46
To discover even more resourceful states… 70
Or continue to being wonderfully unwonderful…

44. Wonderfully Unwonderful!

Here is a fun exercise. Pick a 'negative' state, i.e. one that you sometimes experience but do not really want to feel. For example:

Anger	*Fear*	*Nervousness*	*Anxiety*
Worry	*Sadness*	*Lethargy*	*Demotivated*

Now, take one of the states mentioned above and then put a positive state in front of it (as an adjective). If we take 'lethargy' as our example and then borrow some positive state words from Piece 43. What if you were to feel…

Excellent lethargy?	*Inspired lethargy?*	*Calm lethargy?*
Confident lethargy?	*Blissful lethargy?*	*Contented lethargy?*

How does that affect the state? It may make sense; it may confuse or it may amuse. Whatever it does… it *changes* the state!

What about:

Authentic anger?	*Optimistic anger?*	*Curious anger?*
Calm anger?	*Creative anger?*	*Grounded anger?*

Again, notice how the first positive state changes the meaning of the second state. These are known as 'meta-states'[i]… states about states. And make sure you put the positive in front of the negative because the first word 'governs' or directs the second. The first state mentioned creates a frame around the second state.

One more...

Empowered anxiety? *Curious anxiety?* *Fun anxiety?*
Calm anxiety? *Authentic anxiety?* *Gracious anxiety?*

If some of the combinations still seem negative, change the first word until you get something interesting that (for you) changes or neutralises the original state... or makes it constructively resourceful in some way.

Although any state can be expressed (or suppressed) in an unhealthy way, states *do* serve a useful purpose. Even the so called 'negative' emotions are there to tell us something. For example:

- anger tells us that something is not right and gives us motivation for change,
- fear tells us to be more aware,
- nervousness tells us to prepare,
- sadness tells us that we have lost someone or something important.

To find ways of handling your inner critic... 47
To discover what can create the wrong impression... 72
Or continue to be mindful of your choices

45. *Be Mindful of Your Choices*

"Life is a sum of all your choices."

Albert Camus

Remember that at any given moment, you are making choices. There will always be choices, even when it may appear that there are none. We may feel trapped in a job, a relationship or a hum-drum life, but we *do* have free will. This is the time to focus on what choices we *can* make. Perhaps some people are afraid of the consequences of their choices? Perhaps they feel they are between the Devil and Deep Blue Sea?

The most resilient folk I know focus not only on what is within their control, but also *on the choices available to them*. To be in the driving seat of our own life and career destiny means focussing on the choices we *are* able to make[i].

And if *where you are now* is not working for you... you can choose to make different choices! Everything you do is a choice... including making a *purposeful* choice.

To make the point, consider this:

What are you choosing right now?

For example, what *thoughts* are you choosing right now...

- Thoughts?
- Internal dialogue?
- Frames, meanings and interpretations?
- Feelings, moods and emotions?
- Body language, posture, facial expressions?

- Movements?
- Clothing and appearance?
- Sights, sounds and focus points?
- Behaviours?
- Food and drink?
- Exercises?
- Actions and taking action?
- Activities?
- Goals?
- Tomorrow?
- Short-term and long-term future?
- Environment?
- Places and people to visit?
- Problems, difficulties and dramas?
- Interactions, reactions and responses?
- Relationships and friendships?
- Hobbies?
- Decisions?
- Career?
- Life?

... and what *NOW* are you choosing right now?

"Every day is Choose-Day!"

To focus on what you can control... 19
To discover how to dissolve a dilemma... 107
Or continue to the Zero Point...

46. The Zero Point

Welcome to the 'Zero Point', the moment where we 'stop the world' and the place where we become truly present, experiencing the here and now. In this moment there is no distraction... no internal dialogue. We are in flow... in mindfulness.

The phrase 'Zero Point' is a way of anchoring the 'here and now'. If we are thinking or talking about things that might happen, or replaying things that did, or fantasising about what could or might have been, we are drifting away from the 'Zero Point'. There have been times when I have been out for a walk and realised that I have been yattering away about inconsequential things... and missing the view. Coming back to the Zero Point means enjoying the moment... 'stopping and smelling the roses'!

Internal dialogue (like our sometimes-random conversations) seems to take us in a 'direction' away from being in the here and now[i]. Sometimes it takes us into the future, sometimes the past. Sometimes it is in a constructive direction, sometimes negative and destructive. Sometimes it is a fantasy of what we would like more of, sometimes it is rejection of what is.

1. **Time Direction**: Thinking about the past or the future.
2. **Motivation Direction**: Thinking about what we do not want or want less of (away from) and what we want or want more of (towards).
3. **Relationship Sorting**: Thinking about how things are different or the same as other things.

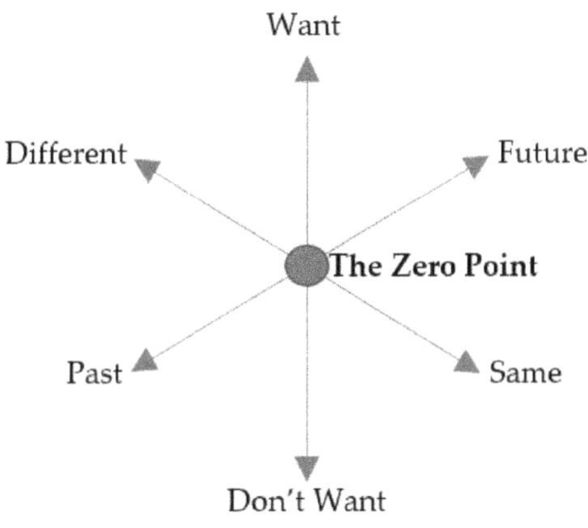

These directions could be imagined as continuums or axes on a graph. The three combined create a three-dimensional X-Y-Z axes model. The *content* of our internal dialogue (e.g. about self, others, things, events, actions) might take us anywhere in this three-dimensional space. For example, we might think about a person we met in the past who we wish we had got to know better because we had so much in common with them. Or perhaps we might not be looking forward to an event that we are going to attend because it will be just like every other event we go to.

The *actual* Zero Point is the centre-point of all the axes. It is here that we are in the present moment, being in stillness and accepting ourselves or what is.

If you take a minute or more to sit quietly and simply observe your internal dialogue, where does it take you? As you become familiar with your own patterns, you can map out where your thinking tends to lead you. It can give you a clue as to 'what is on your mind'!

To find out what to do with the inner worrier… 48
To discover how to 'close the gap' with an audience… 55
Or continue to what to do with the inner critic…

47. What to do with the 'Inner Critic'

Internal dialogue may serve a number of purposes, for example, planning and learning. We might reflect on a situation and when we move through it, we come out the other side with ideas on how to repeat or not repeat it. Research[i] on daydreaming suggests that we have a 'default mode network' in the brain that kicks in if there is not much external stimulus (and/or if we are bored). When this neural system starts up, the brain becomes highly active. We may begin to develop plans and models and have all sorts of creative ideas! It is as if internal dialogue is keeping the brain busy when the outside world is not.

However, not all internal dialogue is positive and constructive. It appears that thoughts run the same neural pathways as spoken language. When we experience destructive language (spoken, thought, heard or read), the same pathways are strengthened in the brain. If the messages are significant enough to set off the 'alarm system' (i.e. the amygdala), then 'negative' thought turns into emotion and physiology. When destructive messages keep running the same patterns in the brain, our body reacts chemically (e.g. adrenaline) and mechanically (e.g. tensing muscles). Under these conditions it is hard work for the body to defend itself against such a constant but intangible threat.

Whilst some of our internal dialogue may be useful and helpful, there may be times when we would benefit from stopping or transforming some of the things we say to ourselves!

We might call this negative internal dialogue *the Inner Critic*... the part that gives us a hard time. Some people are very mean to themselves in their own minds. So, what can we do about it...

- If you had someone standing by your side, saying destructive, unpleasant things, what would you say to them? You might tell them go away (or thank them for their input... and *then* tell them to go away)!
- When you notice the 'inner critic', say inside your mind: "Stop it!" I find this phrase seems to work best when using an assertive but gentle internal command tone. Using an irritated tone seems to exacerbate it. However, you will find what works for you!
- Notice *how* the inner critic is talking... the tonality. What would happen if it was saying the same words, but in a Mickey Mouse or Scooby Doo voice? Would it still have the same impact? Change the tonality so the impact of the words disappears.
- Imagine there is a remote control to control the inner critic... turn down the volume so you cannot hear it any more.
- Ask the inner critic what practical message or feedback it is trying to give you... for example, is it encouraging you to prepare?

To utilise feedback from 'outside' yourself... 50
To remind yourself of your best qualities... 70
Or continue to what to do with the inner worrier...

48. *What to do with the 'Inner Worrier'*

Sometimes, we find ourselves worrying about an impending event... for example, an interview or a presentation. Perhaps we might be feeling anxious about the future or concerned about uncertainty.

The first thing to realise here is that the 'inner worrier' is just a *part* of you that is nervous. It is *not* the whole of you.

Imagine this part of you is like a small child that is frightened and treat it accordingly. How would you deal with a small child that was scared? What if they were just about to get up on stage and they say they are frightened. What do they need and what do they need from you? As a caring and kind adult, what would you say to them?

The best way to handle the 'inner worrier' is to be reassuring. What kinds of things might you say to that anxious part of yourself?

- "It's okay."
- "You are ready."
- "You can do this."
- "Whatever happens you can handle it."
- "You are resourceful."
- "You are strong and creative."
- "Have fun with this… enjoy it."
- "Think forward to later today, when you have already gone through and out the other side."
- "What wonderful things might you learn from this experience?"

- "What a great story this will make to tell your friends!"
- "What might be really funny about this?"

The point here is to find the words and phrases that makes you feel better… safer… happier… readier for the upcoming event.

You are a grown-up. Nervousness and worry come from a child-like *part* of you (the 'inner child' perhaps). Be the best and kindest parent, mentor and guide to your inner worrier.

To address imposter syndrome… 78
To be seen and get heard in meetings… 84
Or continue to the Landscape of Experience…

49. The Landscape of Experience

The Landscape of Experience model is a way of looking at what is happening in the background of our experience as well as in the immediate foreground. It also makes a distinction between our physiology, emotions and cognitive domains (although these three are all part of the same system and not really separate).

As well as giving you nine areas of your experience that you could improve (in order to have a healthier and more fulfilling life), the key to the model is that ***the background has a direct impact on the foreground***.

LONG-TERM BACKGROUND	HEALTH	TEMPERAMENT	PHILOSOPHY
MEDIUM-TERM	CONDITION	MOOD	INTEREST
SHORT-TERM FOREGROUND	SENSATION	EMOTION	THOUGHT
	PHYSIOLOGICAL	EMOTIONAL	COGNITIVE

DOMAIN

Consider your mood and the effect it can have on your moment to moment emotions. For example, if you are in a *contented* mood, you are more likely to notice things that lead to *happy* and *peaceful* feelings. In general, the healthier your background is, the happier your foreground will be.

To improve the nine areas, here is a starting point:

Health	Healthier diet, regular sleep patterns, yoga, structured exercise.
Temperament	Awareness of optimistic & pessimistic tendencies, mindfulness, more outcome focus, keep a diary of 'best things', positive life goals e.g. write a book!
Philosophy	Reframe (seek positive reasons for events), engage with empowering beliefs, plug into your mission/purpose, a spirit of learning/ continuous improvement.
Condition	Meditation, relaxing bath, relaxation activity, exercise.
Mood	Listen to uplifting music, watch/listen to comedy, watch 'feel good' movie, go to positive place/people/context/ environment, tidy the house, change environment.
Interest	Read positive/motivational literature, engage in productive interests/hobbies, help others, get organised and prioritise, complete a task or choose to let it go.
Sensation	Smile, change physiology, breathe.
Emotion	Think about things you love/enjoy, speak your truth with kindness, write down how you feel[i].
Thought	Observe your language and thoughts (positives and negatives), use positive affirmations

To improve your sleep… 113
To understand your reactions to change… 121
Or continue to seeking feedback…

The Third Bit

Pieces About Developing

50. Seeking Feedback

How do others perceive you… and, at any given moment, how good are you at predicting those perceptions? It seems to be quite an artform, getting your predictions as close as possible to how others *actually* see and experience you.

For me, if I *guess* how others perceive me, I think of a range of reactions. Some may think I am interesting and amusing… some may find me irritating and attention seeking! As long as there are more of the first and less of the second, I can cope with that.

There is a paradox here, in that the further we stray from the 'norm', the more memorable we are, but the more likely we are to polarise people's opinions of us. However, if we stick to the norm… we simply become another forgettable face in the sea of faces.

But how do we know for sure what others think of us? The nearest we can get is to ask for feedback.

If you want feedback from someone, give them warning rather than put them on the spot! Be specific about what you are seeking (and why). What do you want to know? What do you want feedback on or about? Do you want to know how you come across generally… are you seen as a 'next level up' candidate? Or do you want to get feedback about a presentation you did or a report that you handed in?

Remember, some people are more elegant and eloquent with feedback… and some are rather clumsy. Some may want to praise you, some may want to give you developmental, 'improving' feedback. Some may give positive but have to add a negative too… they can't help it!

The next part is crucial… what do you do with feedback… how do you handle it? And how do you handle unsolicited feedback (i.e. that which you didn't ask for!)?

1. Thank the other person for the feedback.
2. Ask for more information, perhaps an example. This may feel like the opposite to what we want to do (i.e. get defensive) but actually an example can help you to get a better sense of where the feedback is coming from.
3. Make a decision as to whether to keep the feedback. Feedback is a gift given. Not all gifts are ones you want to wear!
4. What can you learn from this? What could you do differently to implement the feedback and make an improvement?

I have a rule of thumb… if 1% of the population get irritated by something I do (e.g. signing off emails 'Cheers, Joe'[i]), it may be *their* problem (although I *am* still curious about them and would still seek to understand their irritation.) If 99% of the population get irritated, then it **is** my problem! Anything in between, I can address on a case by case basis.

To see yourself through another's eyes… 80
To make sure you look professional on video… 85
Or continue to self-disclosure…

51. Self-Disclosure

Self-disclosure[i] means revealing something about yourself. This can happen naturally as you get to know another person. It could be personal details about your life outside of work. It could be how you are feeling today. It could be your view on current affairs.

However, there are some things that people are 'schooled' into keeping hidden. For example, to realise they are mistaken, to admit that they are wrong, to say how they really feel, to give a truly heartfelt apology when they have behaved badly or said something in the heat of the moment. This can lead to them having a strong 'self-protection' focus... guarded, secretive, armoured, walled, focusing on safety/security and seeking, at all costs, to avoid feeling fear and hurt.

To self-disclose can mean facing some of the dragons of our schooling. It means focussing on 'self-development': personal transformation and freedom, exploring options, developing greater flexibility, being vulnerable, seeking opportunities and feelings of happiness.

When might you use self-disclosure?

- You want to progress
- You don't get/understand something
- You are mistaken
- You are struggling
- You need something
- You feel overwhelmed, uncomfortable, frustrated, concerned etc.

Of course, self-disclosure is a choice… who do you reveal information to and how much do you reveal? To be vulnerable entails risk… and so it needs to be a considered and 'calculated' risk. For example, to reveal that you are ambitious could be useful because it tells someone else you want to progress. However, there are different ways of saying it. For some people, the phrase "I'm ambitious" can feel too bold and perhaps even arrogant. So, listen to the language the other person uses and frame it in their terms. If the bold approach is less likely to work, you might say something like: "I'm looking at next steps… what would I need to do to be ready for when an opportunity arises?" This is couched in the language of humility and curiosity.

To self-disclose and to seek feedback can require resilience and trust in yourself. It also requires openness and empathy. Remember, no-one holds THE truth… it is all data for interpretation and assimilation.

So… to go for it or not go for it? The only thing that can hold you back is your decision not to…

To talk about your impact… 68
To get comfortable 'blowing your own trumpet'… 92
Or continue to the assertive you…

52. The Assertive You!

To be assertive and to act assertively, is to honour your own views, feelings, needs, values and rights *whilst at the same time* honouring the views, feelings, needs, values and rights of the other person/people you are communicating with.

It means standing up for yourself in such a way as *not* to 'step on' or harm others. It is about being direct, kind, honest and respectful.

To help identify what assertive really is… we might briefly explore what is not! Here, we are looking at some of the other behaviours that folks use to try and get what they want in life and at work…

As you can see from the illustration, assertive behaviour is based on high expression and high empathy, i.e. we are prepared to express our own feelings, needs etc. and at the same time take into account the other persons feelings and needs. Aggressive would be high expression and low empathy (expressing self without a care for others). Passive is low expression but high empathy (concerned about what others think, so don't speak up). Indirect is low expression and low empathy (not saying directly how they feel, perhaps hinting, but also not concerned about others).

As someone moves round the 'ring' (anti-clockwise) from assertive towards aggressive, we might say that this would be 'firm assertive' (i.e. standing your ground or speaking up for yourself in a stronger manner). Any further and it simply becomes aggressive and demanding. In the clockwise direction, as assertive moves round towards passive, we might call this 'gentle assertive' (e.g. where we are being kind, reflective and actively listening to the other person).

Being assertive is intrinsically linked to your confidence and self-esteem. When you express yourself cleanly and clearly and genuinely listen to the other person, you are being true to yourself. Even if you do not get the perfect end result, you know you have maintained your integrity.

Speak your truth with kindness!

To be assertive when persuading... 57
To be seen and heard in meetings... 84
Or continue to

53. Put on Your Presenter Shoes!

Good presentation skills can help support your 'brand' and manage how you come across to others. Exceptional presentation skills mean standing out and being remembered for all the right reasons.

You will know you are truly confident at presenting when someone says: "Can you present this?" and your internal response is a relaxed: "Yes, of course, happy to" rather than: "Aaaargh!"

The first step in preparing a presentation is to ask yourself:

- What do I want the audience to know as a result? *(This is as far as most presenters go!)*
- What do I want the audience to **do** as a result? *(If you do not want action as a result, why are you presenting? A call to action will give your presentation a focus.)*
- What might the audience want to know about the topic? *(What is their interest? This will help you connect with the audience, make sure you are engaging them and help you prepare for questions.)*
- What might the audience want to do with their new knowledge? *(How will the audience benefit by listening to you? Again, this will help to engage them and give you confidence in knowing that you are 'giving' them something.)*

The next step is to organise your thoughts into a structure. There are lots of other things to consider here… which is why Melody and I wrote a book called the *Model Presenter*[i]!

However, there is one secret about presenting that almost no-one seems to realise… which will help develop your confidence and handle some of the nervousness…

The audience will only notice about 20% of what you are feeling inside.

The audience has a 'tolerance threshold' for unconscious behaviours (e.g. 'um's, 'ar's and a bit of dancing around!) It is only when a presenter does something more extreme, obvious or repetitive that it 'blows out' the threshold. This is why other presenters often *appear* more confident than we *feel*!

For me, the art of being a presenter and trainer/facilitator is the ability to *handle things when they go wrong*… perhaps with pragmatism, easiness and/or humour. If you want to feel more confident, write a list of things that could go wrong… then come up with at least three solutions (preventions and/or cures) for each concern.

To manage your own state… 43
To deal with being 'put on the spot'… 77
Or continue to find (and fine tune) your voice…

54. Find (& Fine Tune) Your Voice

When you present and speak in meetings, beyond the language you use, your voice and body language will be sending out messages of credibility and connection.

Consider the impact a presenter might have if they:

- Talk so quietly the audience cannot hear.
- Speak at such a fast pace that the audience cannot keep up… or so slowly that the audience lose interest.
- Express themselves in a monotone that makes it almost impossible for the audience to stay focussed.

Quiet voices can come across as lacking confidence. Too fast and the presenter can seem very nervous. Monotone becomes monotonous… boring. What affect might any of these have on a person's image and 'brand'?

Credibility and connection come from a strong, clear, easily audible voice. An expert presenter will utilise their 'voice variability' (i.e. varying the pitch, tone, pace/speed and even volume) to get their message across.

And should we worry about a few 'um's and 'ar's? As long as they are not too repetitive, they can be a gift to the audience! Although the most clinically professional approach would be a deliberate pause, these 'disfluencies' give the brain of each audience member a moment to process what has just been said… and then 'clear the screen' for the next piece of information. No gaps mean no processing of what you are saying.

However, the best way to understand your own 'disfluencies' (which also includes filler words, e.g. 'like', 'so', 'you know') is to record yourself presenting (video or audio). This will help you to become aware of any over-use and then iron them out. It is hard to change behaviours if we are not aware of them. Listening to yourself will also help you get over the "oh, no... is that me?! Do I really sound like that?!" reaction.

Another aspect of voice is accent. Many people I have met say they don't like their own accent and they don't like hearing themselves speak. If you feel that way yourself, remember that you are *choosing* to feel awkward about it. Bottom line... are you clear and understandable to the audience? This is the important factor!

Some speakers do have very strong accents and it can be hard for the audience to process the words. If you have a strong accent, try emulating the accent of your audience... a little. Step in their direction, but do not tread on their toes (i.e. you do not need to copy them)! For example, if you are presenting in French to a French audience... speak French with a French accent.

As a final note... be proud of your accent... it is part of your heritage and your personal history. It can make you interesting and 'exotic'!

To talk about your successes without embarrassment... 92
To discover how to introduce yourself... 104
Or continue to close the gap with your audience...

55. Close the Gap: Get Connected

One of the reasons speakers get nervous when they present is that they feel disconnected and distant from their audience... as if there is a gap in between them that is wide enough for tumbleweed to roam!

This happens when the presenter sees themselves as separate from the group... 'me' the presenter and 'you' the audience. When a presenter connects, they tend to feel as if there is an 'us'... and that 'we' are in it together and on the same page etc.

We call this 'closing the gap' between yourself and the audience[i].

What can you do to close the gap? Here are some ideas for 'in person' and virtual/video conference presentations:

- Acknowledge and welcome folk as they arrive. Smile and greet them.
- Chat to your audience members before you start, particularly if you have not met them before.
- Make eye contact with people around the room. Do a sweep around... I call this the 'lighthouse effect'!
- Mention specific audience member's names and refer to (non-confidential!) conversations you may have had.
- Use plenty of 'you' statements (e.g. "over the next 3 years *you* will find that...").
- Interact with the audience, allow a bit of discussion, questions and answers.
- Get the audience doing something, for example, discussing something in small groups.

- Speak their language… either use their jargon or stay jargon free.
- Fit your solutions to *their* plans, objectives, needs and problems.
- Show empathy to their concerns and challenges.
- Involve the group wherever possible (and where appropriate). Ask for input.
- Tell them the benefits of your ideas in *their terms* and how it benefits *them* and/or the business.
- As a side note on body language, generally, 'palms up' creates more rapport than 'palms down' [ii].

In addition, here are some other ideas for making technical, complex, theoretical or 'dry topic' presentations more engaging:

- Maintain your own enthusiasm, interest and passion for the subject.
- Provide a clear context to what you are talking about.
- Organise data into models, boxes, flowcharts, arrow diagrams, quadrants etc. Use graphics and pictures to show what you are talking about.
- Break it down into manageable, graspable chunks.
- Use metaphor and analogy ("… and that's like…").
- Give real world examples and applications.
- Make meaning out of your data ("… and that means…").
- Use gestures to create pictures.

To learn more about what is important to others… 59
To close the gap when video-conferencing… 85
Or continue to what makes and breaks rapport…

56. What Makes and Breaks Rapport

Behaviours that make or break rapport (and build or destroy relationships) may appear to be common sense. They are not, however, common practice!

We could say that rapport is the behaviour of empathy. The more shared experiences, interests, beliefs, values and goals we have, the easier it is to build and maintain rapport.

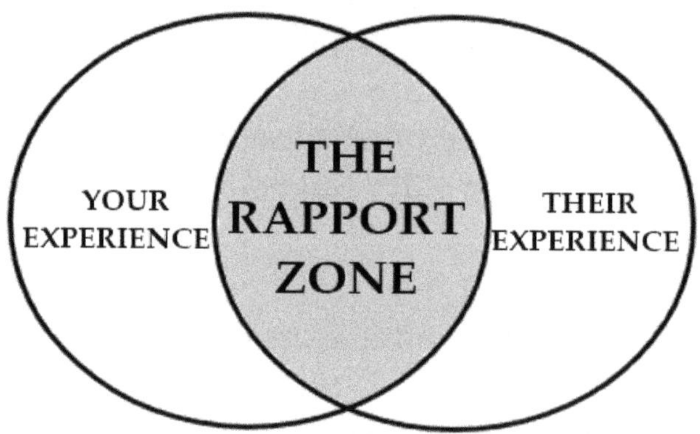

The more we 'match' (i.e. the bigger the 'rapport zone'), the more we 'get' the other person... we like people who are like us (even if we do not like ourselves!) 'Mismatching', on the other hand, tends to break rapport.

Here are *some* examples (as if they really need to be spelt out!) of behaviours that break rapport:

Avoiding eye contact, talking down to others (overly condescending/ patronising), calling them unpleasant or unwanted names, stereotyping ("you lot", "you people"), demonstrating prejudice (sexism, racism, agism etc.), using 'irritator phrases' (e.g. "no offense but" or "with all due respect"), manipulating (e.g. overselling an idea as if it is great for them when it isn't!), lying, breaking promises, disregarding/discounting, arguing, ignoring, putting them down, threatening, not communicating, mismatching values and beliefs (for example: political, social, spiritual, moral/ethical stance... it is probably best to avoid making comments on these until you get to know someone).

And here are some things that build rapport and relationships:

- Smile and be friendly: talk to them as if you already like them!
- Ask them questions about what they enjoy and what they have done. This makes it easier to find things in common.
- Verbally agree with them (when you actually do).
- Give people your undivided attention at any given moment in time. 'Choose to listen' (i.e. prioritise them above any distractions and internal thoughts).
- When appropriate, summarise and paraphrase, to check and show understanding.
- Focus on their concerns and needs: "What do you need?" and "How can I help you?"

To check if you have rapport, subtly observe your body language and theirs... how similar is it? If you are in rapport, your posture, movements and facial expressions will tend to become more and more alike (or 'mirrored'). You can also tune into voice tonality and emotionality... how similar are you (e.g. in levels of calmness or excitement)?

To build rapport with the 'right people'... 89
To explore rapport in interviews... 100
Or continue to the foundations of persuasion...

57. *The Foundations of Persuasion*

When seeking to influence an audience, consider that each person has a 'see-saw' in their mind with 'resistance' against your idea on one side and 'motivation' for your idea on the other:

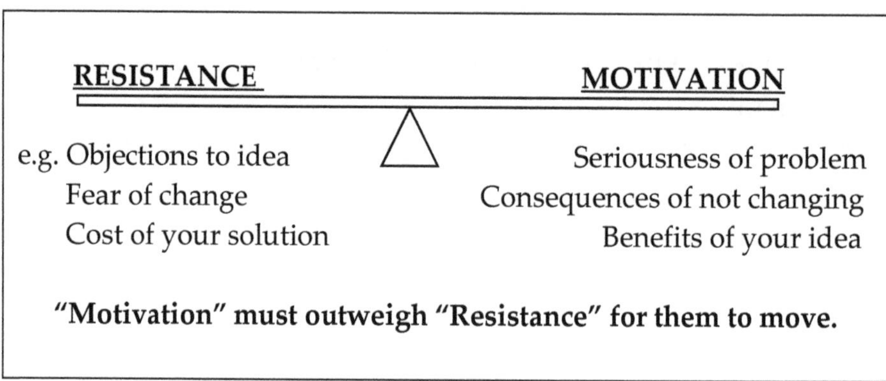

Using the model above, you can plan out an influencing strategy. Start by writing down all the possible resistance you think you might face (i.e. all the objections and reasons 'why not'). Then use that list to write a list of motivators (i.e. why they would accept). Make sure the motivators are in *their* terms (e.g. how it benefits *them*/the business), rather than your own.

An additional approach is to explore how you might move the fulcrum on the seesaw. Move it to the left and it will give you more leverage. What gives you leverage?

- Build rapport with them outside and throughout the conversation.
- Build and maintain your credibility and professionalism.
- Seek common ground.

- Summarise the conversation as you go, particularly on the things you agree on.
- Listen and ask them questions. Pull for more information about their position, perspective, concerns and needs.
- Listen for and respond to their values (i.e. what is important to them).
- Show you are listening, e.g. write down key points.
- Associate what they like to your proposal.
- Appeal to their skills/expertise.
- Involve them in decisions, solutions, plans.
- Demonstrate flexibility in your approach.
- Show enthusiasm for your own idea (and also for *their* input/suggestions).

To focus on ethical persuasion… 63
To learn more about dealing with resistance… 118
Or continue to prepare to persuade…

58. Prepare to Persuade

When influencing, you will need to spend about 10% of your time thinking about you and 90% thinking about the other party. However, in order to get what you want… you need to get crystal clear about what that actually is… and then build in some flexibility! The clearer you are, the more likely you are to get it.

Here are some questions to get you thinking about your case and what you want to achieve (or get):

- What would you like to achieve? If possible, look for a range of favourable outcomes that you would be happy with. Develop flexibility by thinking about your 'WEB'[i]:
  - Worst 'deal' that you would still accept
  - Expect to get (i.e. what is reasonable)
  - Best 'deal' for you (i.e. what would be great to get!) This will be your 'starting position'.
- What would you get by achieving that? (i.e. what are the benefits to you of getting what you want? Might there be other creative ways of getting those benefits?)
- Who, specifically, do you want to influence?
- What do you want the other party to *do* as a result of your influence?
- How will you know that you have achieved what you want? Once they have offered you what you want and have agreed to it… stop influencing and negotiating. Graciously accept!
- What will you do if you cannot get a result? What is your back-up plan? Who or where will you go to next?

- What other information/evidence do you need? You might need to do some research to get you facts straight and 'at your finger-tips'. The aim here is to make sure you are well informed and hence more credible in your discussion.

If you can answer all these questions so that you have focus and flexibility, then you can start thinking more about the other party and what they might need, want, gain from your discussion.

Remember that *sometimes,* influencing can be as easy as simply asking for what you want!

To get clearer about your outcome... 22
To be a positive force for change... 87
Or continue to what is important to them...

59. What is Important to Them?

If you want to build rapport and influence others, it will help you to understand (and utilise) their values (i.e. what is important to them). Our values sit as one of the foundations to our personality, so tread carefully here!

How do you elicit someone else's values?

- Listen to them, what language do they use and repeat? What are they proud of and pleased about?
- Ask them what is important (e.g. how we work together?)
- Check the company website or keep your eyes open to how leadership and teams actually behave and treat each other. If a person or group survives for any length of time, they will *probably* share the company values.
- Listen to what makes them angry, annoyed or irritated. We love talking about things that annoy us! If they are talking about something that people do (or have done) that annoys them, ask yourself: "What is the other person not being?" (e.g. polite, respectful, quick, good enough etc.) This will give you an idea of the speaker's values!
- Listen out for strong agreement with something someone says (using phrases such as: "Oh I agree with you about that", "Absolutely", "Oh, I know what you mean"). Or strong disagreement with something someone says!

Meetings are a great place to tune into values! We reveal our values all the time… it is simply a case of listening out from them!

Here is the secret about values that took me years to figure out! The other person has a set of values. These values will be expressed in a moment-to-moment basis as 'needs'. You have an idea/proposal and this has 'benefits'. If you draw up a list of benefits, it is the same list of words as a list of needs or a list of values. So, sell the benefits of your idea that plug directly into the relevant values of the other person. Their neurons will light up and they will find your idea much more compelling.

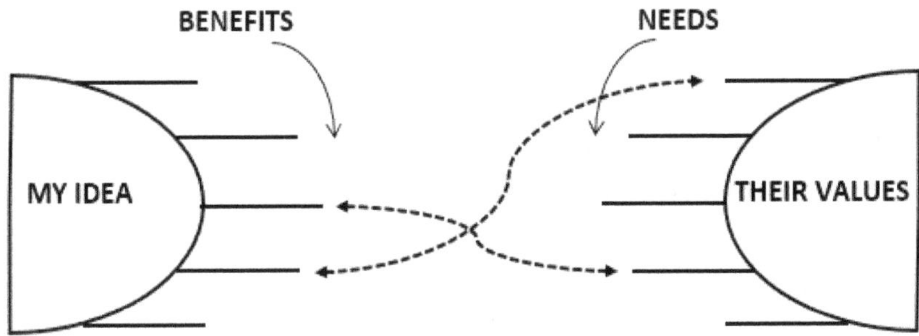

In effect, you are learning to speak their language at the most profound level. And this also applies to how you communicate up and down the business. What is important to the senior management team will often be different to what is important to the front line (e.g. those dealing directly with customers.) Tune into the needs and concerns at each of the organisational levels and pitch your ideas accordingly.

To demonstrate organisational level values… 83
To deal with difficult behaviours… 116
Or continue to making your case…

60. Making Your Case

Imagine that everyone goes around with a full mind. It may not always look that way, but go with me on this one!

When proposing an idea, it is helpful to start by 'creating a gap' in the mind of the audience to create space for your idea. A 'gap' might be in the form of doubt or mild psychological discomfort with the present situation. If you do not create a gap, your idea may simply pour out over the edges and get lost.

The following formula is an approach (though, of course, not the only approach) to make sure you create a desire for change before presenting your proposal:

The Cons & Pros Formula

1) Context	*Where are we now? (Evidence based/factual)*
2) Concerns	*What is not working with the current situation?*
3) Consequences	*What could happen if nothing changes?*
4) Proposal	*What are you proposing?*
5) Profits	*What are the benefits/gains of your proposal?*
6) Process	*How would you implement your proposal?*

As much as possible, put you case forward in *their terms* (i.e. as to what is relevant and important to them). If they are more senior, put it in terms of the business, if they are nearer to front line, it will be more about personal gain. It is *not* persuasive to put it all in your *own* terms (i.e. how it is a problem to you and how it would benefit you if they changed!)

It is essential that your first few statements (i.e. about context) are evidence based and factual. You need to start in a way that the audience cannot disagree. What you are saying is self-evident or backed up by their experience or by the published figures. By starting with fact, you place your flag in the sand. As you move through your proposal, you will tend to become more selective and focussed with the information you present and the interpretation you put on it.

Finally… and this is important! Spend roughly 20% of your time on the 'cons' and 80% on the 'pros'. The 'cons' section is simply there to set the scene, create a gap and demonstrate a need. If you spend too long on the 'cons,' your message will become swamped in 'problems' and you risk coming across as 'being negative'. The idea is to create a bit of dissatisfaction with how things are now (in order to get them to move), not depress them to the point where your solution does not bring them out the other side (i.e. feeling positive and motivated about your idea).

Think of the 'Cons and Pros Formula' as a shallow U-shape… take someone who is content (but blissfully unaware), make them uncomfortably aware… and then make them happily aware and motivated by the end!

To talk about your achievements… 69
To handle a lack of direction from others… 123
Or continue to how to get a salary increase…

61. *How to Get A Salary Increase*

Getting an increase in salary is not always the easiest task. The trick here is to get clear about a number of key factors. Any or all of these could provide enough 'leverage.' You will need to be convincing and you will need evidence and back up data.

Without wanting to put you off, it is *essential* that you have a realistic case to make. Too many people simply assume they *should* get a pay-rise because it is 'owed to them' or that they are 'due it'. This is an example of a 'fantasy-reality gap'[i].

Here are some key factors in getting a salary increase:

Research the System

- **Equality**: What are the industry averages for your job role/level? How about others in your company – are you on the same pay as others doing what you do?
- **Influence**: Who is the decision maker? Who has the power to say 'yes'? If this is not your manager, is it possible to get to the decision maker via your manager? If not, consider how you might set up a meeting with the decision maker to make enquiries about salary.
- **Precedent**: How does a pay rise happen in your company? Who do you know that has done it? Offer to buy them a coffee and then ask them how they did it!

Think About What You Bring to the Party

Experience: You need to demonstrate that you are a 'safe pair of hands' and that you are useful to the organisation. Perhaps you have been with the organisation for a long time and so have greater knowledge of 'how things work'. Remember however, that no-one is truly non-expendable, so do not overstate your case (nor rely on experience alone). Also, don't expect a pay rise after a couple of months of starting a job (unless that was part of your original contract).

Responsibility: Can you take on tasks and activities that are at a higher level of responsibility than your current job role? If a significant percentage of your job shifts to higher responsibility, you could make this part of your case. However, don't expect a pay rise if you are simply doing more work... long hours doing more of 'what you do anyway' are rarely rewarded with pay rises.

Value: Demonstrate your worth to the organisation by showing where you add value. Think about your job (particularly any extra activities you have undertaken) and ideas for improvement you have had (and perhaps implemented). Where might you have saved or made the company money because of your ideas, input and skill? Think beyond simply what you do (action)... what are the results of your action (what have you delivered?)... and what are the bigger picture impacts of those results (i.e. what does it mean to your department/company – what are the organisational benefits of improvements you have made?)

To build your brand awareness... 71
To develop your organisational level thinking... 82
Or continue to understand the political game...

62. *Understanding the Political Game*

Even if you don't want to play the political game, it is still useful to understand it. Unless you run the show, you cannot necessarily control the game… but you *can* control your part in it... as long as you know what to be aware of.

There are two main ingredients in the political game: **ethics** and **intelligence**. Often, politics are associated with the unethical, manipulative and devious behaviours of those Machiavellian hobnobbers that may (or may not) be controlling things from behind the scenes. Many folk are not interested in political shenanigans, as it all seems to be too much effort… particularly when there is plenty of real work to be getting on with.

If you are reluctant to get involved, here is an easy guide to handling company politics (without necessarily needing to play the game!)

Firstly, consider the ABC of progression (see piece 66): do a good job, make sure the 'right' people see you in the 'right' way and build your connections.

Secondly, it is possible to be ethical AND develop your organisational intelligence. Here are some examples:

- Be thoughtful about your actions, but be prepared to stick your head above parapet. Expect criticism from those at the same level and below. Although this might seem hurtful at first, develop your resilience. Work with the criticism. Assess it as feedback… evaluate the credibility and motive of your critic, take any useful bits on board and choose to set aside the unhelpful or destructive. Take it as a sign that you are progressing and stepping up.

- Choose to keep on developing. Ask yourself: "what else could I do?"
- Seek to develop your ability to 'scope' (i.e. to take a big picture view *and* drill down into specifics when required)
- If you are a manager, as well as promoting yourself, speak also about your team's achievements.
- Seek a mentor, a role model… and offer to be a mentor to others.
- Promote the positives… talk about what is going well.
- If something is not going so well, recommend changes. If something is not liked or is perceived as unfair then talk about ideas for making it better
- Seek to build and maintain connection and credibility.
- Work smart… what are the small things that make a big difference (i.e. minimum input for maximum return).
- Manage priorities, boundaries and expectations.
- Collaborate with others and be empathetic.
- Seek to integrate ideas. Be a connector.
- Make your primary focus 'us' (i.e. others and self).

To develop your organisational intelligence… 81
To prepare for success and its effects… 109
Or continue to being impeccable…

63. *Being Impeccable*

When I talk about 'being impeccable' here, I mean being 'above reproach'... acting in a manner that we are 100% satisfied with.

Being impeccable links to:

1) Assertiveness: You are expressing your needs and also empathising with the other person's needs; acting in a 'win/win' manner and speaking your truth with kindness. Here is an 'assertive check' question: *In acting this way, am I truly respecting the needs and rights of the other person as well as my own?*

2) Integrity: Acting with integrity means simply: acting congruently with your own values and beliefs. Integrity does not mean that you are objectively right! Indeed, someone could behave in a harmful manner towards others and still be in alignment with their own beliefs and values. In terms of an 'integrity check' question, you might ask yourself about an action: *Would I feel 100% happy if someone did this to me?*

3) Ethics and morals: If you are doing something or going to do something, is it ethical? An 'ethics check' question might be: *Could this action cause harm to any other person, the company or the environment?*

4) Ecology: Be aware of the 'ripple effects' of your actions. What impact does it have on others... and how might they perceive you if you act in a particular way? An

'ecology check' question might be: *If I did this, could it lead to any negative side-effects for me or others?*

Here are some examples of behaviour that tend to fall short of being impeccable:

- Talking about someone who is not there in a detrimental manner, without their knowledge or permission (i.e. 'gossiping').
- Hiding something from someone that could cause them trouble or harm.
- Sharing rumours and conspiracy theories without properly checking the credibility of the source.

Being impeccable might mean:

- Apologising for mistakes or poorly chosen words in our communication.
- Keeping agreements and promises. Delivering by the agreed time.
- A 'repair' or 'refund' if someone is not satisfied with what we have agreed to do for them.
- Contributing or giving feedback only to improve a situation.
- Checking facts and sources before making claims.

If you want to be perceived as impeccable, make sure any agreements you make with someone are clear and 'nailed down'... then stick to your side of the 'contract'.

To explore the assertiveness angle... 52
To rethink how you view 'being employed' ... 73
Or continue to get realistic about time...

64. *How to Get Realistic... About Time!*

Consider the past month. Some of your time will have been spent doing things you planned to do (known as Proactive tasks). The rest of your time will be spent doing things that 'crop up' (known as Reactive or Responsive tasks). The things that you couldn't plan for might be highly productive (e.g. a new business enquiry) or distracting (e.g. a sales call or a colleague talking about last night's TV).

Now... what percentage of your time was actually spent on planned tasks... and hence what percentage was spent on the things you couldn't plan for (no matter how important they might have been)? I call this percentage split the Re%Pro[i] formula.

As soon as you identify your typical Re%Pro, you can be more realistic about how long planned tasks will *really* take. For example, if your split is approximately 50/50, you need to allow 2 hours in the diary/calendar for a 1-hour task.

Here's a chart to give you an idea of how long tasks will really take you:

Reactive %	Proactive %	1 Hours planned work will take...
0%	100%	1 Hour
10%	90%	1 Hour 7 Mins
20%	80%	1 Hour 15 Mins
25%	75%	1 Hour 20 Mins
30%	70%	1 Hour 26 Mins
40%	60%	1 Hour 40 Mins
50%	50%	2 Hours
60%	40%	2 Hours 30 Mins
70%	30%	3 Hours 20 Mins

75%	25%	4 Hours
80%	20%	5 Hours
90%	10%	10 Hours

Obviously, you can get more planned work done by taking yourself away from the reactive environment (or removing reactive events e.g. switching off your emails/mobile phone) for a while. However, if you are 'open for business', expect planned work to take longer and with Re%Pro, you can be a little more scientific as to how much longer!

The Re%Pro formula can help you drop the fantasy of how much work you *might* get done, and deal with the reality of how much time you are *really* likely to have available. This should also encourage you to prioritise more effectively. If your job is roughly 50/50, then you only have half your time to focus on your to-do list (e.g. 20 hours in the week rather than 40). Therefore, do the tasks that give you the *best* return (and/or prevents the most hassle you would receive if you did *not* get them done!)

In addition, be aware that when you take on a new task or action… you will need to run that through the Re%Pro formula too. For example, if you take on a task that (uninterrupted) should take two hours… block out more than that in your diary to account for the reactive 'stuff'.

To take time to broaden your connectivity… 91
To overcome the issue of 'not enough time'… 110
Or continue to pathways to progression…

The Fourth Bit

Pieces About Progression

65. *Pathways to Progression*

First things first… there is more than one way to progress your career. If you are thinking only of promotion, you may need to broaden your view. Waiting for your own manager to move on could be a long waiting game! If you do like the look of your manager's job, ask yourself: *What is it about their job that appeals to me?* Write a list. Now ask yourself: *what other jobs/roles might give me those things?*

Here are some examples of different progression pathways:

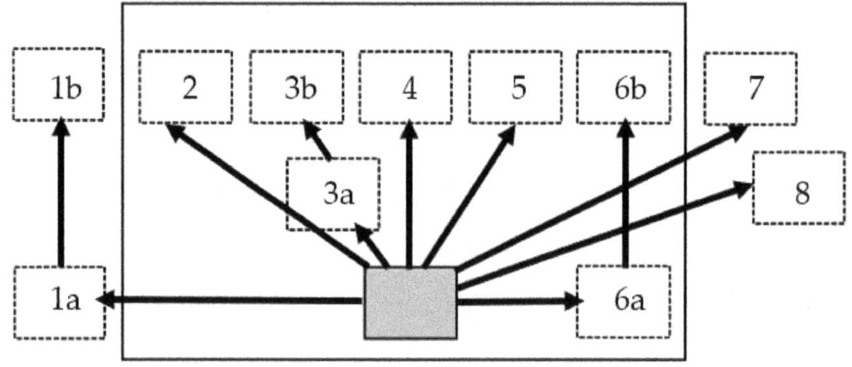

1. Get a similar job in another company with better progression prospects.
2. Move diagonally up in your company to another more 'senior' role.
3. Take a stepping stone job get you to the next level above. Or 'act up' and take on more responsibility (not just more tasks), to develop your role. Then seek to upgrade your job-role.
4. Get promoted.
5. Create a new job in the organisation where you see an unfulfilled need.
6. Move sideways in the company to get a broader experience to then move up.

7. Seek a step up in another company.
8. Start your own company!

These are just some ideas to get you thinking. How have you progressed in the past? Does it fit one of the patterns above or was it a different journey? Of course, if you like the company you work for now, you might go out for a while to get your step up… and then return later.

If you have a good relationship with your manager, make sure they know you are interested in progression. It will then depend on how supportive they choose to be. Be ready for them to seek to maintain the status quo (i.e. you continuing to do what you do!) You may need to *make* time for career related conversations if your manager does not *give* you the right opportunity.

When having the conversation, here are some questions you could ask:

- When a promotional opportunity arises, what would I need to do to be ready for that?
- What would I need to develop?
- What would need to happen to develop X?
- What can you delegate to me in order to help me develop X? (And ask yourself: what can *I* delegate and to whom?)
- I need your help and support to take that next step. What do you need from me?

To be your own career coach… 18
To deal with career blockers… 114
Or continue to the A-B-C of progression…

66. The A-B-C of Progression

This majority of this *Bit* of the book is focussed on three key areas which become the A-B-C of progression:

- Achievement
- Brand
- Connectivity

For the sake of our purposes here, we might define or describe these three things as follows:

<u>Achievement</u>
Your achievements are those things you have delivered and completed with a good result. This is where you have demonstrated your value and worth to a company. It could include qualifications, performance, completed activities/projects, successes and wins.

<u>Brand</u>
Your brand is how you portray yourself… a combination of how others see you and how you see yourself (i.e. your self-image and confidence). It is related to how you are perceived, remembered, talked about and treated. It is your reputation… being remembered for the *right* reasons!

<u>Connectivity</u>
Your connectivity is about visibility… who that matters, knows what that matters, about you. Those with connectivity know a lot of people and a lot of people know them. In other words, they have a strong network.

You will find that positive Achievement is a good platform on which to build Brand… and then your Brand is the platform for Connectivity. It is easier to create a positive brand if you are an achiever…. And it is easier to build your network when you have a strong positive brand.

A classic example of *mis*-managing the *ABC* would be a member of staff (at any level) who is performing and making improvements (i.e. *Achieving*), but is not informing/updating their manager (i.e. no *Brand* or *Connectivity*). They are managing the reality (*A*) but not the perception (*BC*) of their work. If the manager does not know that something has been improved, they will assume it is still the same as before (hence, even the *Achievement* is not acknowledged).

If you have been *achieving* things… you need to find a way to let your manager know so that they actually hear you! What is the best form of communication *for them*? What do they respond to best… email, memo-note on their desk, face to face? Let your manager know the results of what you have been doing and the positive impact it has had. This will help to develop your *ABC* with the next level up.

To explore your brand… 71
To develop your connectivity… 88
Or continue to why some people do not progress…

67. Why Do Some People Not Progress?

"I've had years of achieving my objectives...
but still not got promoted."

Not everyone wants to progress, and this is probably just as well! However, there are plenty of folk who would like to be more successful but who don't seem to make it.

This brings us back to the theme of the book... *how to take control of your career.* Too many people are in the passenger seat, waiting to be noticed. They perform well and then wonder why they are getting overlooked for promotion. Even worse, they may see others getting promoted who are not as good as they are!

Here are some explanations as to why some people do not progress... to help you make sure that *you* get into the driving seat instead:

1) There is a principle known as the 'good student model'. Through school, college and university, our success is measured on our performance, achievements and results. Then, we enter the world of employment and that model does not work so well any more.

2) Look at it from the manager's perspective... if someone is good at what they do, why would the manager want to let them go?

3) Are we giving off mixed messages of want it/don't want it? Are we actually being clear that we want to progress?

- Some give off signals that they are not happy and do not want to be where they are now… but they don't communicate clearly enough what it is that they do want. It is as if they are 'hinting at' their manager!
- Some say they want to progress but then they don't take action to get it (e.g. not prioritising it, doing their normal job but not pushing for the new developments).

There is a general rule of thumb[i] that successful progression is down to about 10% Achievement, 40% Brand and 50% Connectivity. However, most employees seem to focus 95-100% of their attention on Achievement and 0-5% on their Brand and Connectivity. This does not mean spending 90% of your time on Brand and Connectivity, it means understanding how success works.

Do not expect your achievements to guarantee you getting noticed. Make time to get yourself 'out there' and 'noticed' by the right people.

To determine your career focus… 17
To overcome a lack of direction… 124
Or continue to action-results-impact…

68. Actions-Results-Impact!

To achieve is to deliver results… to perform… to meet or exceed your objectives… to make things happen… to keep your promises… to fulfil your responsibilities…

To achieve, you will find it useful to be: organised, focussed, hardworking, dedicated, current and educated/skilled in what you do.

It is admirable to be the best *you* in whatever you seek to achieve in life and career. It can give you a sense of purpose and something to be proud of.

However, you also need to think beyond your to-do list and actions… to the results that your actions have led to, i.e. what you have delivered and what the end product was. Then you need to consider what impact (bigger picture ripple effect) this result had on the business. What was the bigger benefit? What did it mean to the business?

When we tell others about our achievements (assuming we do at all), we tend to say what we have done or have been doing. Whilst this may feel great to tell someone how busy we have been and relay to them our entire to-do list, it may not be interesting to them! Especially if we are talking to senior managers. They may not care that we have *done some things*… that is what we are paid to do!

If someone asks you (even casually): "what have you been up to?", think beyond your to-do list. Instead of talking about actions, talk about results (i.e. what you delivered) and the impact that has had (e.g. to the service, customer, project, department, organisation as a whole). If this feels to much, you can couch it in terms of: "I'm really delighted, having completed my marketing campaign, it has attracted over 100 new customers!"

Think of this as your 'return on investment' for the company. What value are you adding? Here are some examples:

Team Benefits (AIM)

- Achievement (e.g. innovation, ability to achieve more, efficiencies and making something 'easier').
- Interaction (e.g. improved communications, clarity and direction).
- Mood (e.g. motivation, improved team morale and reduced conflict/tensions).

Organisational Benefits (PIE)

- Performance (e.g. profits, savings, cost preventions, efficiencies and competency).
- Image (e.g. commitment to staff, attracting talent and enhanced company brand and recognition).
- Engagement (e.g. customer satisfaction, retention or growth, increased morale, staff satisfaction, low staff turnover and keeping knowledge in the business).

To explore other ways of making your case… 60
To find other ways of promoting yourself… 92
Or continue to the achievement tracker…

69. The Achievement Tracker

It is important that you have a mechanism for recording and keeping track of your achievements. Most companies have some sort of annual review process, so imagine being asked now: "What have you done over the past year?" Would you have a full answer? Most people cannot remember what they were doing last month, let alone eleven months ago! Life is busy and time passes on by…

Here is a simple and yet powerful tool to help you keep track of your achievements. I call it… The Achievement Tracker!

At the end of every month, use a table/spreadsheet to type up what you have achieved. If you are being measured by objectives (and company values), relate your achievements to your objectives and behaviours to the company values:

What have I done this month to ***deliver*** my objectives?
What have I done this month to ***demonstrate*** the values?

	January	February	March	April	May	June	July	August	September	October	November	December
Objective 1												
Objective 2												
Objective 3												
Objective 4												
Objective 5												
Value 1												

Value 2												
Value 3												
Value 4												
Value 5												

By keeping a track of your good performance and helpful behaviours, you will then have a rich source of data to talk about at your annual review!

This can also help you to 'embed' the company values and get a stronger understanding of how they translate to your job role.

In addition, you will find that the examples you write down will (a) give you a sense of accomplishment and (b) be an excellent source of examples for answering interview questions.

To explore setting objectives and goals… 22
To find out more about organisational values… 83
Or continue to your resource pot…

70. Your Resource Pot

If you are seeking progression, going for interviews or simply want to feel good… you might consider creating a 'Resource Pot'.

The Resource Pot is a combination of your achievements, strengths, motivators and joys. These things combined can help to enhance your self-esteem, self-worth and self-regard.

As you write things down, think of some real-world examples of where these things are (or have been) true. This can be useful for interviews where you will usually get asked for examples and evidence of what you have done. Part of interview preparation is to think of questions you might get asked and then come up with answers. It is much better to have a load of examples ready, rather than having to think about them spontaneously in the stressful environment of an interview.

In addition, when you talk about the things in your resource pot, your enthusiasm and confidence is more likely to shine through naturally.

To help you fill in the pot, here are some more specific questions.

Achievements

- What have you delivered, made happen, organised, published, completed, won, participated in…?
- Where have you exceeded on your objectives or on expectations?
- What are you proud of?

Strengths

- What are you good at, what are you confident at?
- What have you learnt and mastered?
- What are some of your best qualities?

Motivators

- What gives you a buzz, lifts you or moves you forward in some way?
- What is important to you (e.g. about your job)?
- What does that (e.g. job) give you?

Joys

- What are your main interests/hobbies/pastimes?
- What do you enjoy, what is fun, what enthuses you?
- What makes you smile and brings you happiness?

For each of the items on your combined list, think of/write down at least one specific, real-world, tangible, measurable example as evidence of your brilliance!

To gather more resources from your story... 33
To explore how to use your resources for interviews... 96
Or continue to your brand awareness...

71. Your Brand Awareness

Your brand is about how you present yourself to the world; do you stand out or do you blend in (to the background)? Of course, both options may be appropriate at different times. Indeed, you may want to find a synthesis… i.e. to fit in *and* be noticed.

Your brand starts with how you see yourself. How strong is your self-image? How confident are you with other people and in what you do? How much do you trust yourself… to be able to deal with what a situation might throw at you?

Your brand is also about how others see you. How influential are you? How valuable? How compelling? Do others know that you are trustworthy? Do they know about your expertise? What first impressions do you create… apologetic, humorous, light-hearted, serious, grumpy, professional?

Your brand needs to be seen and experienced over time. How do you develop your brand? Who do you 'hang around' with? Are you the person that other people want to spend time with? Rapport is connected to your brand and develops with each encounter we have with a person; and hence there are layers of rapport. You will have different levels with different people: some who you would be happy to work with, to chat with, to spend lunchtime with, to socialise outside of work with, to be good friends with…

You need to be remembered for the right reasons… not the wrong reasons! Have you noticed that some folk wander around in a grimace of their own making? Do not be that person! Check the mirror from time to time; check yourself when video-conferencing. How do you look? How is your posture? Do you look your best? You don't need to be a narcissist, just be aware of how you look!

Pedantic though it might be, I would encourage everyone to work on their grammar and spelling; no matter how hard that might be. Trust a 'perfectionist' colleague (or even the writing-app corrector) if that helps. Unfortunately, judgements tend to be made about the poor use of spelling and grammar.

Folks will also tend to make judgements about your appearance, how you dress, your hair… and that is just for starters! Sad but true… we do judge the book by its cover when it comes to others. Dress appropriately but choose how 'eccentric' you might want to be. Make a statement by all means… as long as that statement is not 'leave me alone'!

Of course, we also make judgements about what people say and how they say it. So, if (in a particular situation) you have nothing positive or constructive to say… consider saying nothing! Do not make 'the best speech you will ever regret'[i]!

To remind yourself about connection and credibility… 7
To develop your rapport building… 56
Or continue to what creates a 'wrong' brand…

72. What Creates a 'Wrong' Brand?

Whilst the premise of this book is to focus on the positive and constructive, there is nothing wrong with being aware of what 'wrong' looks like. This can help you to navigate the potholes and pitfalls of your own personal brand development!

Consider the impact of the following examples of behaviour and attitude:

- Being negative and cynical. Focussing on what is wrong and why something will not work.
- Being sceptical without good reason.
- Complaining.
- Being argumentative.
- Bullying others (e.g. threatening physically or psychologically, name-calling, overt prejudice or discrimination).
- Gossiping and talking about others behind their back.
- Delivering poor quality work.
- Not delivering and not keeping promises.
- Making excuses without rectifying.
- Defending mistakes instead of owning up and putting it right.
- Being consistently late.
- Not taking care of one's appearance. Looking 'scruffy' and dressing down when everyone else looks smart.
- Poor personal hygiene (and that includes the tricky subject of body odour, which aside from some rare medical conditions is generally avoidable).
- Making sarcastic, pointed or cutting comments designed to put the other person down or 'in their place'.

Each of the above examples will tend to make the 'wrong' impression. If somebody exhibits enough of these behaviours and qualities, they are likely to be branded and remembered as 'difficult' and someone to avoid.

Even if you are angry with someone, disappointed with a decision, not feeling listened to or believe that you have 'seen it all before', there are more constructive ways to influence the situation and express your feelings and views.

Have a look at the list above and add your own examples. Then double-check yourself. Do you ever do any of them? If you do, what are you trying to achieve by doing that? How else could you achieve that in a more constructive way (i.e. that builds your brand positively)?

To understand more about bias... 38
To develop a positive online presence... 79
Or continue to employed means self-employed...

73. Employed Means Self-Employed!

Whether you are employed or self-employed, someone is paying you for your service. That 'someone' is your customer. If you are employed, consider that your employer is your customer... how does that change your perspective? In this sense, you are like a supplier or an 'internal consultant' delivering a long-term project. You might be 'self-employed' with the same company for years!

Being self-employed carries risks as well as benefits. But, whilst there are technical and legal differences, why not gain the psychological benefits of being self-employed... even when you are employed! So, what are the benefits?

- You tend to feel more in control of your own destiny.
- If a job is not a good fit or does not add anything to your brand, then you can seek another customer.
- You are responsible for your own joy!

If you are a consultant, you have to bring your 'A' game all the time. Your continued work depends on the customer valuing what you do. What else does a consultant need to do?

- Do something unique that others don't appear to do so well.
- Recognise and look after you brand.
- Take ownership of your development.
- Stay plugged in to what is happening in the market place.
- Get good at 'shmoozing' and networking.

- Stay motivated – every day, you are delivering something and making a difference.
- Be proud of your product (i.e. you).

Can you do the above whilst technically being employed? Yes, of course. Does this make you a better employee? If it makes you a happier, more motivated and more resilient member of the team… then yes!

If you imagine yourself as a self-employed consultant, how might that affect how you feel about your work?

To determine if you are in a state of readiness… 15
To create a positive impression in a new job… 125
Or continue to your legacy…

74. Your Legacy

When you leave a room, how do you want to be remembered?

After an interaction with someone, how do you want them to think and feel about you?

What would you like to be known for within a specific department, organisation, association, group or environment?

If people talk about you to others, what do you want them to say about you?

The answer to the above questions may be different depending on the context; or it may be the same throughout.

Here is an exercise for you: Write down three qualities or characteristics that you would like to be known for.

Consider your three answers. For each one:

- What would that look like?
- What behaviours would reflect those qualities?
- What might you need to do to be perceived that way?
- What might you need to stop doing?

These questions are not designed to make you self-conscious and 'act' a particular way. You still need to be you… but expanding on your repertoire of behaviours.

These questions *are* designed to help you take control of your brand and your legacy (i.e. what you leave behind). You cannot make others see you a particular way because they will be looking at you through their own filters. You might want to be perceived as humorous; but others might perceive you as a joker who does not take things seriously! However, you can 'invite' them to see you how you would like to be seen. And you do this by behaving consistently and congruently to your desired legacy.

On the simplest level, I like the idea that when someone meets me a second time, they have a positive feeling inside and they think: "oh good, it's Joe" (or some such!) rather than a sinking feeling and the thought: "oh God, it's Joe"!

If it helps you to crystalize your own thinking, here are three of the legacy qualities I aspire to:

1) *Light-ness*: To me this refers to light-heartedness, humour and 'light-bulb' moments. I enjoy it when people say that they feel 'better' as a result of a conversation with me, that they feel clearer about something and/or they go away with new ideas.
2) *Smart*: As well as humour, it is important to me that others understand that I know my stuff, that I have credibility in my knowledge and in my application of knowledge. Despite a bit of eccentricity, I also like to be called 'dapper' in what I wear!
3) *Real*: This is, in part, about being perceived as down-to-earth, grounded, pragmatic and realistic but also connected, 'sorted' and straightforward. I want folks to know where they stand with me!

To explore how your legacy is part of your story…33
To be a positive force for change… 87
Or continue to assess your confidence…

75. Assess Your Confidence

The word 'confidence' comes from the Latin meaning 'with trust'. When we are confident, not only do we gain trust from others (i.e. we appear more trustworthy), we also trust ourselves. This is important! When we are confident, we trust in ourselves to be able to handle situations. We know that whatever life throws at us, we will deal with it.

Think about a skill you have or a thing you do where you are totally confident. The likelihood is, whatever might happen, you will have a way of dealing with it or you can trust yourself to be able to improvise. When we are not-confident, we lack these strategies.

Here are three approaches that will help you to feel more confident.

1) ***Contingency planning***: If you are preparing for a specific event, ask yourself what could go wrong and then for each issue, come up with some solutions. If necessary, get advice from other people.

2) ***Increase the amount of strategies you have for handling situations***: You can do this using the 'IBO' Model (Intention-Behaviour-Outcome). In any given situation, get clear about your **Intention** (what is it you are trying to achieve) and then consider a range of **Behaviours** (strategies) that could help you get what you are trying to achieve. Finally, for each Behaviour, check the possible **Outcomes** that might have. Make sure you have at least three to ten different **Behaviours**.

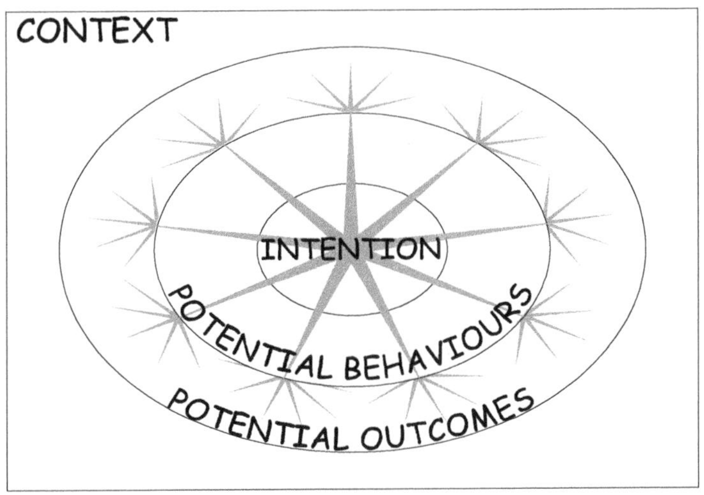

3) ***Practice reframing***: Before you jump to conclusions in any given situation, make sure you have thought through a *range* of frames/ways of interpreting what might have happened and/or what that might mean. We tend to be more relaxed and confident when we can explain what is going on in a number of different ways. If someone ignores us in the corridor and we have only one interpretation of that, we might end up feeling rejected. However, if we have six different reasons in our mind as to why someone ignored us in the corridor, we tend to be more philosophical. We are also more likely to check with the other person to find out if they are okay.

To explore another model of reframing… 39
To apply confidence to uncertainty… 122
Or continue to access your confidence…

76. Access Your Confidence

Would it be valuable to you to become *more* confident *more* often… to be able to switch it on when you need it?

Confidence is a psychological and physical state. You *feel* it! How do you know when you are confident? What is it like for you? Where do you feel it? What is the intensity level? How does it move in your body… from your core outwards, upwards, downwards or does it loop around?

Where would you like to be (and feel) more confident in your life? What would be an example situation? There are areas of your life where *you are already confident*. You know what confidence feels like! And if you go to one of those memories or places now… and feel what it is like to be on top of things and in control of what you are doing… and as you feel that, what do you notice about that situation where you would already like to feel more confident now?

Different things can drive your confidence, for example:

- Your posture. Whether you are sitting or standing, notice what happens when you raise your sternum (breastbone) about an inch upwards. Your shoulders go back, your head comes up and your breathing is fuller. If you are standing, notice what happens when you place both feet firmly on the ground… solid and strong. I call this your 'Confidence Stance'.

- Music. You know how music can shift your state almost immediately. Write a list of songs, soundtracks or

> instrumentals that raise your spirits. Those tracks, that when you hear them, make you go: "Yes!" inside. The songs that make you want to get up and dance (even if you choose not to!) These are the songs to play in your head when you need them.

Of course, we also don't want to become over-confident. Nervousness serves the purpose of making us prepare and take something seriously. Confident people still prepare and plan... then they trust themselves to handle (and even enjoy) a tough situation. Those that are over-confident become arrogant and complacent, pretending that they don't care. Remember, over-confidence may sometimes get a person hired... but it will also probably be what gets them fired!

To play with how you can be confident... 44
To deal with your 'inner critic'... 47
Or continue to spontaneous confidence...

77. Spontaneous Confidence When Put 'On the Spot'

There are times in meetings, presentations, training, negotiations, interviews and conversations where we may get put on the spot. Typically, this is where we are asked a question that we don't know the answer to or cannot answer easily.

When we feel 'put on the spot' (e.g. faced with a tough question), we need to get back in the driving seat to remain calm… and hence stay confident. We cannot always prepare everything… so I designed this model (Directions of Thinking[i]) to help give you a sense of the many directions you could go and hence give you a number of options (even when, initially, you don't appear to have any!)

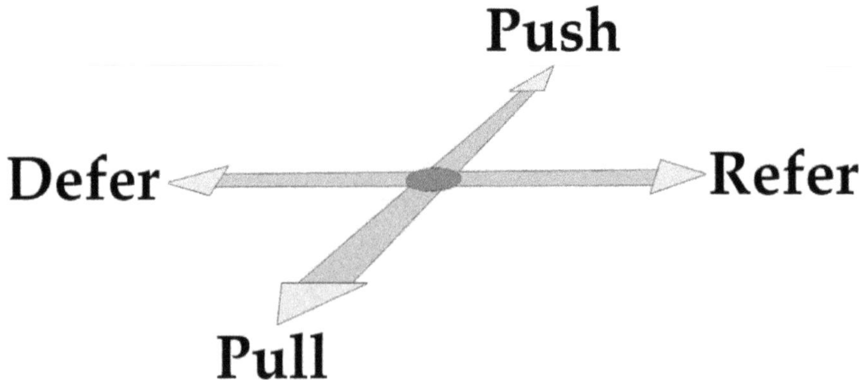

Push: *Give* information, an answer or propose an idea.

Pull: *Draw* information from them. Ask a question or ask for more information about what they are looking for. You could ask for an example of what they are asking or clarification of what they mean.

Defer: *Delay* your response. Utilise time. Say you will have to find out and come back later, or that you are happy to discuss that outside the meeting, or say you will need time to think.

Refer: *Source* your information... an expert, an authority/ decision maker, policy, procedure, law, research... Tell them who they need to speak to or say you will speak to them.

Remember that you will always have some different 'directions' you can go... and hence multiple options of how to respond in a given situation. Think of the model as an 'arena' in which you can move around... so you might, for example, push **and** defer at the same time.

You can also use this model to plan or generate new ideas for 'next time': "If I'm in that situation again, I could..."

To explore the persistence/flexibility combo... 10
To consider some tough interview questions... 99
Or continue to addressing imposter syndrome...

78. Addressing Imposter Syndrome

Most folks experience imposter syndrome at some stage or another; some more so (and more often) than others. It can be specific contexts that set off feelings of doubt and inadequacy, or being with certain types of people.

The 'imposter' is a deceiver, a confidence trickster, a front, imposing themselves on others. They are not what they seem and may not really belong. And anyone who suffers from 'imposter syndrome' tends to be afraid that, at any point, they may 'get found out'.

Imposter syndrome can be a result of our comparisons. For example, comparing our internal state (e.g. of doubt) with another person's external appearance (e.g. of confidence). What a strange situation then, that when a group of people come together, many of them will be looking at others and thinking: "They all seem more confident than me!"

Remember, you are not alone if you are feeling that way. Others may be feeling (or will have felt at some point) like the imposter in the group. I know lots of Chief Executives that have felt that way!

Where does it come from? Usually childhood, picking up disparaging messages from parents and teachers, designed to 'put us in our place'. Children should be seen and not heard… that kind of thing. Then later in life, although we are apparently 'grown up', we find ourselves in a room full of people who *really do* seem grown up… and they appear to know what is going on and what to do… and so that 'little kid' part of us is triggered… and everyone else comes across as so much more competent and confident that we do!

However, consider the following as a 'cure' for feeling 'less than':

- Others may be feeling it to… but we cannot tell because we can only see about 20% of what is going on inside someone else[i].
- Other people may be jealous of *you*… because you come across (to them) as being so confident!
- If you have 'internal dialogue' telling you that you are no good, whose voice is it? What would happen if that person's voice sounded high pitch and squeaky, like Micky/Minnie Mouse? How much power would it have then?
- Seek the **confidence** exercises elsewhere in this book. When you embrace your true confidence, you don't need to feel like a confidence trickster!
- Feeling like an imposter is usually the *first stage in a process* of settling into a role. We move from doubt to willingness to learn, to developing more strategies… to greater confidence.
- Everyone has their own strengths and development areas. No-one is objectively better than you.
- Remember you bring something to the party that others may not bring.
- You have value and you add value. There is a reason you are here. You serve a purpose. You are enough.

To deal with your internal critic… 47
To be prepared for success… 109
Or continue to your online presence…

79. Your Online Presence

How do you manage your online presence... particularly with social media? If you 'ego-google' (search yourself), what do you find? What images does your name bring up on a search engine?

Remember, if you are going for a job, your online presence is an open book. So, how are you presenting yourself to the world? What comments and opinions have you put out there? What kinds of things have you said to and about others?

What photographs are linked to you? Your picture is your visual legacy. Out of context, a series of stills can provide an interesting profile of a person. We cannot help but make judgements about others based on how they look, how they dress and what activities they are involved in. How do you want people to see you?

I was at a conference some years ago and someone took my picture standing next to a flipchart. In the spur of the moment, I did a kind of superhero pose and put on my catalogue model face. It seemed funny at the time. The person published the picture and there was a couple of comments saying that I looked arrogant or that I looked like a fool! A shame. They didn't even know who I was or that I was fooling around. Of course, it could have been worse, but it was a gentle reminder. What may seem 'cool' or humorous to me may look foolish to someone else! Of course, we cannot pander to the whole world and what they might think... but we do need to take responsibility for how we present ourselves.

What if you would rather be the person holding the camera than the person having their picture taken? Whilst many people are comfortable with having their photograph taken, others seem to produce an awkward 'rictus grin' when a camera is pointed at them.

If you want to look more natural in photographs, the tip I learnt is to laugh whilst your picture is being taken… as if something mildly amusing just occurred to you… or that having your picture taken is funny. Whilst it may take a bit of practice, this tends to create a more natural, photogenic smile[i].

And finally, if someone takes a picture of you that you do not find flattering, ask them to delete it or remove it if they have posted it online. It is your right to do so. Of course, it does not guarantee they will remove it, but they certainly won't if you don't ask.

To consider if you are starting a business… 16
To raise your brand awareness… 71
Or continue to see yourself through another's eyes…

80. See Yourself Through Another's Eyes

We live, most of the time, in the 'shell' of our head, looking out from the inside. Aside from the occasional glance in the mirror, we rarely see ourselves from another person's perspective. Even the mirror is a reversal of what we actually look like.

In the age of video-conferencing, we see ourselves more regularly, there on the screen with a bunch of others. However, we don't tend to notice ourselves when we are in the flow of conversation. We are more likely to be looking at others. If we do catch ourselves in 'listening mode' it can make us self-conscious to the point of not doing much at all!

What we are talking about here is 'self-awareness', closing the gap between how we think others see us and how they *actually* see us. Apparently, we are not always great at knowing how others think and feel about us… how they place us... and what labels (positive, negative and neutral) they might have for us.

How often do you see video recordings or hear audio recordings of yourself? Many people prefer to avoid such things, acting squeamish, embarrassed or shocked by their own appearance or voice tonality. "Is that really what I look like? Do I sound like that? I hate seeing or hearing myself speak!"

If you find it challenging to see/hear yourself from an external perspective, I encourage you to get your mobile phone out, point it at yourself and talk about something you know a bit about! Talk to the camera as if you are presenting a television programme. Then watch it back (with the sound on!) When you can do this and seeing/hearing yourself becomes a normal and neutral experience, then you can stop! A video of yourself is the best feedback you will ever get.

The trick is to set your defensive filters to one side and give yourself permission to watch and listen. Give yourself constructive feedback on what you like (or what is okay) and things that you would like to improve and get better at.

Remember, the best presenters in the world started somewhere... and responded to feedback in order to improve.

This is not about being liked, loved and adored by all people. It is about knowing, understanding and accepting the range of experiences you might engender in others.

To ask for feedback effectively... 50
To reduce nerves when presenting... 55
Or continue to your organisational intelligence...

81. Develop Your Organisational Intelligence

How much do you know about your organisation? Who are the key players and influencers? Do you have your finger on the pulse? What is happening in your market place and where does you organisation sit within it?

Organisational Intelligence is not just about understanding the 'organogram' or hierarchy tree of the company you work for, it is also about understanding who are the movers and shakers… and are you perceived as being be one of them?

Have a think about how much you know and how well you could answer the following 'practical' questions:

- What do all the other departments do?
- What are some of their challenges?
- Where do we sit within the marketplace? How are we perceived?
- What major projects are going on?
- What does the organisation need from me?

And what do you know about the following 'influence' questions:

- Who does what and who knows what?
- Who is doing what with whom?
- Who has power and influence (and who influences them)?
- How well do I know these people? What do I know about them?
- Where is the power? What kind of '-ocracy' best describes your organisation? For example:

- Democracy (power in equality and relationships)
- Meritocracy (power in results and talent)
- Autocracy (power in authority and leadership)
- Plutocracy (power in wealth and money)

Having an organisational focus means understanding what is going on beyond your own job. The more senior you are, the more you are expected to grasp this. This means being aware of the successes and challenges within the business. Each of the different levels will have their own types of issues, concerns, questions and needs.

It also means learning the 'language' of other departments and other levels. If you need to influence or put forward a proposal, you need to do so in *their* terms and according to *their* needs.

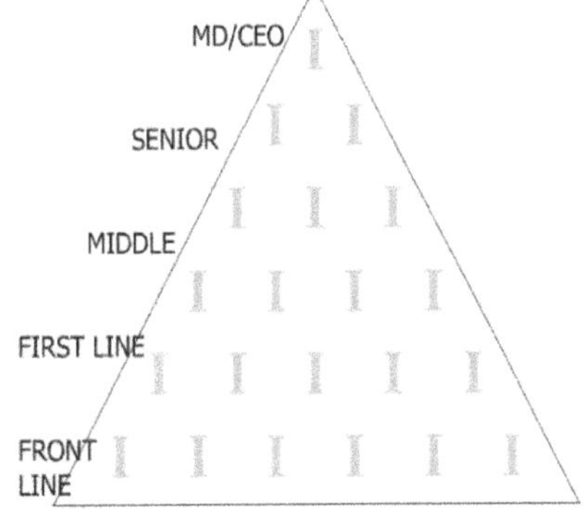

To prepare for some strategic influencing… 58
To focus on approaching the 'right people' 89
Or continue to organisational thinking…

82. Demonstrate Organisational Level Thinking

Imagine meeting a senior manager in the coffee area. They ask you a question like:

- How are you doing?
- How are you getting on?
- What are you working on?
- What have you been up to?

How you respond will determine how you are perceived! Many will respond to these types of questions by outlining their recent 'to-do' list… i.e. what they have done. Unfortunately, this is not of great interest to most senior managers. Telling them what actions you have taken is simply like describing your job description to them.

What may be of more interest is the results you have had, the outcomes, the things you have delivered and what you have achieved.

Even more interesting to the senior manager is the impact that you have had on the business. If you have done something, what was the result and how did this benefit the service, the department or the organisational as a whole? You can do this without having to 'blow your own trumpet', e.g. "I'm really pleased... we've just completed project X and we now have customer Y on board and ready to work with us…" or "I'm rather chuffed, I got feedback that the workshop I ran last week led to an innovation saving us £50K." Of course, these things need to be true!

Think: *Action – Results – Impact (ARI)*

Listen to the language of those more senior than you. What is important to them? How do they impress each other? Be prepared to talk about cost savings and return on investment! Be prepared to network upwards (and outside the organisation). Understand your company's role/place/position/image within the marketplace.

By talking about the bigger picture, organisational view (rather than simply focussing on your own job), you are speaking their language and addressing their needs and concerns. They are more likely to perceive you as one of them or at least 'up and coming'... ready to fast-track perhaps?

Get comfortable with power and responsibility... but beware: organisational level thinking is more *disassociated* and *detached*. So, stay plugged-in to the other levels of the company. Do not lose touch with the 'front line'. No matter where you are in your career, always remember to do the walkabout, chat to the teams and thank the cleaner! *Stay human.*

To understand more about self-disclosure... 51
To think more about your presentation skills... 53
Or continue to demonstrate organisational values...

83. Demonstrate Organisational Values

In an organisation, there is usually a published set of values. These will perhaps be on the website, the company intra-net and perhaps pasted everywhere about the building. If you work there, you may be appraised according to those values.

On the surface, values can appear a bit fluffy and vague. However, they sit above (and should drive) a set of behaviours. If employees are only measured and evaluated by their performance (but not behaviour), this can lead to more unproductive behaviours (e.g. bullying) as folks tread on each other in trying to achieve their objectives and get a better bonus. This does not really engender teamwork! And if any bonuses are reliant only on team performance rather than individual, you will find some folks will pull their weight but feel that they are dragging the weight of other team members too. When people are not rewarded for their personal merit, this can lead to 'social loafing'... where some members of the team take their foot off the accelerator and then coast along. Hence, values are important to give us a sense of 'how' to go about things, not just 'what' to deliver.

So, what are the published values of your organisation? How are they defined and described in the company literature and materials (which could be online)? What examples are given in terms of behaviours that would fit the values? How would you demonstrate that you are meeting the values and how do you record that?

In addition to the espoused, published values, there may also be some unpublished, unspoken rules and values. These are important too if you want to understand the underlying game being played in the company. Of course, you still need to demonstrate the published values, but you will also want to be mindful of what goes on under the surface! It may be that these additional values can help you get noticed and progress.

Here is a set of questions that may help you to see the unspoken values in action:

- What other behaviours (beyond those published) get measured, monitored and evaluated/judged? What are people *being* (i.e. what values are they demonstrating) when they are *doing* those behaviours?
- Beyond the published values, what else seems to be important to the company?
- What behaviours get rewarded, praised, respected and commended?
- What behaviours do others seem to 'get away with'? And who is able to do this (e.g. certain levels of management, certain 'people who know people')? Is there one rule for some and another rule for others?

Observe those who 'get on'. How do they go about things, i.e. in what manner (e.g. with humour, cheeky smile, directness, indirectness, empathy, under the radar, up-front, involving, putting themselves forward…)? Test these behaviours carefully and subtly. If only managers senior to you can get away with certain behaviours… then take care that you are not seen as 'too big for your boots'!

To find a company that reflects your values… 36
To explore the benefits of mentoring… 90
Or continue to being seen and heard in meetings…

84. Being Seen and Heard in Meetings

Meetings, particularly those with key influencers in the room, can be a useful place to shine… or at least to get a sense of who thinks what, who expects what and who is making decisions (or influencing the decision makers).

How do you want to come across in a particular meeting? How do you want to be perceived? If relevant, what messages do you need to get across?

Some people seem to think that they have to dominate the air-space in order to show their influence and leadership, but there are other ways of creating credibility in a group:

1) *Content leaders*: Being an expert in your field, you can speak with authority about your experience.
   - What is your level of credibility? If others do not know your credibility, ask smart questions (e.g. "what, if anything, would stop us from [your idea/proposal]"?)
   - Build credibility: Speak confidently, refer subtly to your experience/expertise (e.g. "over the past x years, I've been working with…"), utilise the authority in your role/position (e.g. "as the health and safety manager, I suggest we…").
   - Do not just say: "I like x", explain why: "I like X *because…*" [give evidence and examples].
   - Demonstrate the benefits of your own ideas… What's in it for *them* or the business if they accept the proposal?
   - Identify consequences of bad ideas: "Just so I understand, what would happen if we did x? How would that impact on y?"

- Number or label reasons/benefits (e.g. "there are four key reasons why…").
- If you like what someone else says, voice agreement… even if it is for only a part of what they say. Be an integrator: "What I like about your idea is…"

2) *Process leaders*: Even when you cannot input into the content/discussion, you can input onto the process (i.e. how the meeting runs).
   - If there is a decision to be made, help to clarify the criteria – what would a good outcome look like?
   - Summarise (particularly if things are a bit stuck): "Can I just check… we have an agreement on a, b and c…". Be an *unofficial* note taker. Recap order/processes/actions.
   - If you have enough credibility and things are off track, you could refer to time.
   - Mediate disagreement – show people where they *do* agree, even if they appear not to (e.g. "it seems that you both want the project to succeed…")

3) *Psychological leaders*[i]: Even when you are not speaking, you can demonstrate leadership.
   - Build connection: Make eye contact with speakers, demonstrate you are listening.
   - Nod and make appropriate agreeing noises. *Those with power in a group are more active, even when they are not talking.*
   - Stay calm, focussed, empathetic, assertive and attentive.

To make your case in a meeting… 60
To understand more about handling conflict… 117
Or continue to video conferencing…

85. Video-Conferencing

It is amazing how unprofessional many folk look when they are sat, hunched over their laptop and using video conferencing for meetings, coaching, training, presenting, interviews and online networking.

From technical issues (not knowing how to use the platform, speaking whilst on mute or freezing with unfortunate facial expressions) to unflattering (or indecent!) camera angles, lighting and proximity to the screen. Then there is the messy office or kitchen behind them or an array of weird digital backgrounds… which can create a bad visual effect. Add to this: other people wandering by in various states of dress or undress, children screaming, dogs barking, doorbells and phones ringing.

Some meeting attendees, when video-conferencing from home, don't always dress professionally (including not bothering to wear trousers/skirt!) Some folks forget they are on camera; and hence they itch and scratch and pick at themselves!

So, what might be some best practice? Please note that some of this may seem obvious, but it is all based on real-world experiences of apparently professional participants!

- Get familiar with the technology/platform that you are using.
- Dress for work. You are working!
- Create a professional background. For example, a blank wall or bookshelves work well. If you have no other option but to use a computer-generated background, get

a green-screen (though even this can look weird when the individual moves or picks up cups).

- Make sure the lighting works for you. Natural light is best, but not behind you. Test it out and make your best judgement.
- Have your camera on the screen you are looking at. Some people have two screens and are constantly facing away from the camera. Adjust the height of your laptop/camera so when you look at the screen, it looks like you are making eye contact with everyone else. If necessary, sit back a bit. Make sure your eye-line is in the top half of the screen, with the whole of your head visible.
- Have your device (laptop/phone/tablet) in a stable place… not on your lap!
- Pay attention to whoever is speaking (as you would in an 'in the room' meeting). It is so obvious when so called 'participants' are checking emails or looking at their phone!
- Have your video on and you microphone on mute unless you are speaking or involved in an active conversation.

To be and hence appear more confident… 28
To focus on making a good impression… 102
Or continue to the credible thank-you…

86. The Credible Thank-you!

Some cultures will thank you for doing something and some will not. Indeed, in some places, it could be considered offensive! It is a tricky subject, so get to know the cultures you work with. This is the same with organisational cultures... some will promote the idea of acknowledgement and some will not.

In the UK and USA (for example), 'thank-you' is part of 'good manners'. It is a way of acknowledging that someone else has done something for you, helped you or given you something. It might be a thank-you in passing as a person opens the door for you, or it may be a more official thank-you for supporting a project or going the extra mile in some way. The thank-you in passing can help to maintain an image of politeness (and can prevent some folks from getting annoyed at your rudeness for ignoring them when they took the trouble to open the door for you!)

The 'credible thank-you' is when someone has gone the extra mile for you and you want to acknowledge that. Where and how can you do that? And who do you acknowledge it to? Obviously, the person themselves... and how about their manager? If you are their manager, then flag it up to *your* manager. Is it appropriate to mention it at a team meeting? Is there a way of recording or publishing the thanks in some way (e.g. staff newsletter, company intranet)?

Why would you thank other people if no-one is thanking you? Here are a few reasons:

1. When you publicly thank others, you will also get noticed. A credible thank-you raises *your* profile.
2. The thanker is in a position of power (even if a small amount). Why are you thanking them? Because you were leading or managing something, delivering something… and they helped you? What did they help you with? (E.g. "I'd like to thank Anna for her support which helped us deliver project X on time.")
3. Thanking others is within your control, being thanked is not. If you wait for others to thank you (in order to be noticed), you are not in the driving seat. If you get a public thank-you, then that's great… but don't expect it.
4. If your organisation does not have a thank-you culture, then you are promoting one. An organisation is a group of individuals who may have forgotten 'thank-you' (e.g. because they are too busy). An organisation is also a system and systems do not 'care'. It is up to the people to bring the humanity… and if you don't do it, who will?

As an aside, have you ever received a hand-written card or note of thanks. Have you still got it? Many recipients keep those notes for years! If appropriate, when you are offering others a credible thank-you, consider a handwritten note rather than the generic email.

Over a period of time, the person who gives credible thanks will raise their own image. If you publicly thank a person for genuine reasons, you will raise your odds of being noticed.

To remind yourself about connection and credibility… 7
To create good impressions in a new job… 125
Or continue to be the positive force for change…

87. Be the Positive Force for Change

Gandhi is credited with the phrase: "Be the change you want to see in the world". This also works within an organisation.

Have you ever heard a person saying things like: "this organisation is no good at…" or "the problem with this place is…" or "this organisation should…"? What kind of image does that create? How will those people be perceived and labelled?

To develop a positive brand, recommend positive changes when things are not working, not fair or not right. Rather than complaining[i], be the change you would like to see. Develop simple solutions to move the culture in a more constructive direction… even if it is only at the level of your own team. Communicate your ideas and make it easy for others to follow. Take action and lead by example.

Talk in positive terms about your team. If you are the manager, sort out issues at the local level (unless they need to be referred or escalated), but promote the successes of your team to your own manager and in meetings. Within the team, ACT (Acknowledge, Celebrate and Thank) on successes and exceptional effort!

When it comes to the organisation, your department or your team[ii]:

- **Acknowledge** any faults or any differences. Where necessary and possible, change things to make improvements, influence others to make changes, adapt to those things you cannot control or influence.

- **Accept** that no organisation is likely to be 'perfect' according to your personal ideals, standards and values. It is what it is! Be philosophical about the 'imperfections' – indeed sometimes this is where the gems may be mined. There *will* be differences, but these can provide alternative perspectives and become a crucible for innovative ideas.
- **Appreciate** what your team, department and/or business does, for example, in helping others for a greater good.
- **Admire** other individuals, teams, departments, leaders for their qualities and skills.

If you cannot accept, appreciate and admire the company you work for or the people you work with… you may need to find somewhere where you can.

It is interesting to see and hear how employees identify with their company (or not). An indicator of dis-engagement is when staff talk about 'the/this company' or even worse, about 'them'. Some like to talk about their company as a name (e.g. "Acme has a great approach to solving problems…"), which could be disengaged, but could also indicate a sense of pride (you have to listen to the tone of voice). Those that are more engaged tend to talk about 'us' and 'we'. I have also noticed a flip point in middle-management where a manager shifts from talking about 'the company' to 'we'. If you like the company you work for, and you are talking to an influencer… make sure you are one of 'us'!

To be the 'right person' at an interview… 94
To make the best of change… 119
Or continue to connectivity…

88. Connectivity: The 'Right People'

Who, that matters, knows what, that matters, about you? How can you get seen by the right people in the right way at the right time? How else can you get your name out there and talk to individuals you don't normally talk to? (Both within the company and outside).

Where do the 'right people' hang out? The coffee point, the kitchen? Take a moment to visit there from time to time. For example, if they are mixing at the coffee area, make sure you 'bump into them' (though be careful of going overboard as that could seem like corporate stalking!)

What does the 'in-crowd' talk about and do beyond work? For example: what cars they drive, what sports events they go to, what leisure activities they get involved in (e.g. golf, cycling)?

What if you get invited along to an event? Even if you do not play e.g. golf, you can still enjoy the experience e.g. meet them at the 19th hole. You don't necessarily have do what they do in their spare time… just remember and show an interest in what they are doing e.g. if a 'right person' is playing golf at the weekend, then ask: "How did the golf go?" You only really need to know enough to ask questions.

Build a picture/table/spreadsheet/spider-diagram of your 'right people' network[i]. This is like a stakeholder analysis for yourself and your career:

- Who inside/outside the organisation could have an influence/impact on your future? Who could be influential (and expand *your* circle of influence)? Who could help you develop and progress? This might be a specific person you know (or know of) already. If it is a job role (e.g. CEO of company X), then find out the person's name.

- What is your current connection? What do they know about you? What do you know about them and their interests? How strong is that connection? How easy is that person to access? (This will be on a continuum from good connection to perhaps no connection.)
- How can you forge and strengthen each connection? Most experienced folk are happy to give advice if asked. Indeed, it can be flattering. However, *do not only contact people when you want something from them*! What can you give back (e.g. a link to an article they might find particularly interesting?)
- When the time is right, how can you make it clear to them, in an appropriate and acceptable manner, that you want to progress?

Get to *know* the 'right people', do not just sell yourself at them!

To broaden your connectivity… 91
To get more comfortable with networking… 101
Or continue to approaching the 'right people'…

89. Approaching The 'Right People'

When approaching an influencer, make sure you have a reason to contact them. Create a reason if necessary (without lying, of course!) Indeed, why are you talking to *them*? What do you have in common (e.g. a shared experience/interest)?

I think of this reason as a '***gateway***' into the conversation. For example:

- Were you in the same meeting?
- Did you hear them speak at a conference?
- Was it recommended that you speak to them? And if so, by whom? Do you know someone that knows them? Are they happy to recommend or introduce you?

What exactly are you going to say to introduce yourself? For example:

- "In the meeting this morning, I had a couple of questions about something you said…"
- "I understand that the project you managed has been really successful. I'm looking to get into project management myself. Can I ask you a couple of questions about it?"
- "I was talking to Freda this morning and she recommended I speak with you…"

Get crystal clear about what you want from the conversation. What are you trying to achieve and why?

If you are looking for help with progression, one way is to book a brief meeting with a 'stake holder'. You might say something like: "I've been thinking about next steps for my career and I'm really interested in what you are doing. Could I book 5 minutes with you to ask you a couple of questions?"

Alternatively, you might get to know them a bit (i.e. build some rapport!) and then, when you are with them at a quiet moment, ask your questions.

Or you might seek them out and say: "There's something I wanted to ask you about... is now a good time or can we book a few minutes?"

Here are some example questions:

- I'm interested in being a [job role X]. What kind of opportunities tend to come up?
- What would I need to do to be ready for such opportunities?
- If anything does come up, how would I find out?

To explore your role in making luck happen... 12
To interact effectively online... 106
Or continue to the benefits of mentoring...

90. The Benefits of Mentoring

Being a mentor can be hugely rewarding, helping someone else develop and learn from your successes (and non-successes!) If your company (or professional body) has a mentoring scheme, it is also a great networking opportunity for you, meeting other mentors and developing your own skills through mentor training programmes. Being a mentor is also a boon for your C.V.

Being mentored can serves two purposes. Firstly, the right mentor will help you develop skills and competency so that you will be performing at the top of your game. Secondly, a mentor may be able to provide you with opportunities to raise your profile and thus your exposure and connectivity.

If you want to seek a mentor (or more than one!), you might need to take a formal or informal route. A formal approach would usually be through a mentoring scheme in your organisation (or professional body). The question then is how might it help you and how could you access it? An informal approach would be to ask someone specific to mentor you.

If you intend to seek a mentor, formally or informally, get really clear about what you want from them. Contract with them how often and for how long you could meet. Show interest in 'shadowing' to see how they approach meetings, presentations, negotiations etc. Before any meeting you might have, write down some questions. Your mentor might address them (if they are able to) or they might have other things they want you to explore. However, by being prepared, you can take responsibility for co-driving the relationship.

What qualities might you look for in a mentor? Here are three examples:

- **Reliability.** This may seem obvious, but if you have a mentor who keeps cancelling on you (or worst still, does not show up), then you may be dealing with someone who is either too busy to be a mentor or someone who isn't valuing/prioritising the mentoring process. Either way, it may be time to look for someone else.
- **Direct vs non-direct.** Some mentors will talk about their own experiences. Some may show more interest in who you are, what you do and what you want to achieve (perhaps seeming more like a coach in some respects). They might get you doing something and then ask you to self-reflect. Or they might tell you how they think you did. So, what are you looking for? A mentor who is more directive or non-directive, or a bit of both?
- **Perception vs reality.** Not only will they give you advice, practical tools, tips and ideas that you can use, a good mentor will help you shift your perspective on areas where you may currently be limiting yourself. They may challenge you but always with a view to helping you to become more confident (as well as competent).

To develop your readiness for opportunities... 13
To use mentoring to understand the political game... 62
Or continue to broaden your connectivity...

91. Broaden Your Connectivity

Be a Joiner and a Volunteer!

One of the best ways of keeping up to date with your profession is to join your relevant institute or association and get along to any local, national, international or online events and conferences. Professional events are also good places to network. You never know who could be an influencer in and on your future.

You might consider going further than this: if your professional body has a local branch/group committee, it is worth looking at volunteering and joining that committee. Firstly, it means you have more influence and authority, but it also makes attending events and networking easier. As a committee member, you have a role (i.e. checking other attendees are okay, introducing them to others or simply chatting to them to make them feel welcome). This should give you more confidence in approaching and talking to people at events.

Beyond volunteering for a professional committee, here is a list of other things you could put yourself forward for (both within your company and outside). Some may appeal to you (and your skills) more than others:

- Get on courses (in house and external) to meet a broader base of potential connections. Take an active role in your learning.
- Get yourself a mentor.
- Offer to be a mentor.

- Be a speaker. Offer to present at meetings, events and conferences on your area of expertise.
- Be an editor (e.g. of a newsletter or intranet news). This gives you permission to talk to anyone in your company.
- Volunteer for organising committees, action groups and projects that could raise your profile.
- Seek opportunities to take a leadership role.
- Contribute effectively and constructively in meetings.

To get into a state of readiness… 14
To build your online network… 105
Or continue to blowing your own trumpet…

The Fifth Bit

Pieces About Action

92. Blowing Your Own Trumpet!

If given the opportunity (e.g. in a presentation, a meeting or interview) to: "tell us about yourself," what would you want others to know about you in 30 or 60 seconds?

There are various philosophies on this, ranging from the pragmatic to the 'spin'. Pragmatic means telling them what you do and how long you have been doing it. This can come across as a bit 'samey' to everyone else. The 'spin' means telling people the benefit of what you do. The cliché here is 'sell the sizzle, not the sausage'. However, this can leave others a bit confused about what you can actually do... and it can sound either pretentious or evasive.

A best of both worlds approach might mean answering some of the following questions:

- What is your role?
- How long has this been your field?
- Main qualification (if relevant)?
- What is your purpose (i.e. you do what you do in order to what?) How do you support others? How do you support the business? (E.g. if you are in I.T: "I help teams to be more efficient, and hence save the business money.")
- If relevant, what is your key value? What is most important to you in what you do?

Obviously, it depends on who you are introducing yourself to. Speak their language and make your role relevant to them, i.e. how/when they would interact with you and/or use your service. Consider their 'map' and put it in their terms.

As mentioned elsewhere (Piece 82), if you are talking about achievements (e.g. at interviews or performance reviews), consider the following:

Action: What are some examples of things you have done/achieved recently?

Results: What was the outcome of those actions/ achievements?

Impact: What was the bigger picture (team, department or business) impact?

When invited, be prepared to 'sound the trumpets'... but don't go on about it. Like a trumpet solo, it is good to know when to stop!

To draw from your resource pot... 70
To develop your networking prowess... 103
Or continue to the flexible CV...

93. The Flexible CV

If you are applying for jobs, your CV may be the first point of contact. The specific requirements of CVs will change over time (according to the fashion), however, there are a few points of best practice that are less likely to change.

As with application forms and interviews, the recruiter is looking for you to answer three key questions:

1. **Can you do the job?** And how well will you do it? How skilled, experienced are you and how much potential do you have to learn?
2. **Will you do the job**? How motivated, enthusiastic and passionate are you?
3. **Will you add value?** How will you complement and make a positive difference to the team (and to the company)? What special skills & qualities do you bring?

Where possible, check what the company wants from you. If they require a particular style or layout or type of content, then this will supersede any of the following tips:

- **Language & Length**: This is perhaps the most obvious one to start with. Make sure that all the language in the CV is positively stated, constructive and is outcome oriented (i.e. about what you have achieved). Keep it to two sides of A4 (and check the grammar and spelling). Stay factual and true. Give examples and figures.
- **Personal Profile**: At the top of a CV there is usually a summary of 'who you are' and 'why you'. This part of the CV needs to be tailored to the specific company you are applying to. Seek out any of their value, vision and

mission statements. Look at their website, what type of language do they use? Look at their social media presence, what do they claim and promote? Use some of their key terms (but avoid simply cutting and pasting!) If the company claims to be innovative, then show how you are innovative. If they say they are traditional, show how you are traditional!

- **Experience:** This section, about the companies you worked for and the job roles you held, will only need to be tailored to the specific type of job you are applying for. Make sure you are demonstrating the technical knowledge and potential to do the job. Use "I" not "we".
- **Qualifications:** This depends on where you are in your career. If you at the beginning and looking for a starting point job, then give the relevant qualifications with levels and grades. Qualifications show that you are capable of focus, self-discipline and study. If you are further on in your career, you will probably only need to give any 'higher' education and professional qualifications.
- **Interests:** Perhaps optional though it gives a sense of who you are beyond the workplace. Always good to mention any voluntary work you have done and any positions of authority you hold/have held in recent years. If you put something unusual, consider the impression it portrays and then be prepared to answer questions (unapologetically) about it at the interview stage!

To build your C.V. from an achievements' tracker… 69
To consider some possible interview questions… 98
Or continue to interviews: being the right person…

94. Interviews: Be the Right Person

An interview is an opportunity to assess and evaluate the company as well as them assessing you. Have confidence in the fact that the interviewer may be just as nervous as you… because they are under pressure too! They have the onus of *finding the right person* as much as you have of demonstrating that *you are that right person*!

So, as far as they are concerned, who *is* the right person? In a nutshell, they want someone who will show up, deliver and add value. They also want someone with potential to develop and grow within the company. What they want to *avoid* is getting the wrong person… which then means more costs in terms of recruitment and tribunals if they end up selecting a 'problematic' employee.

To be considered the right person, you will therefore need to demonstrate and answer the 'ASK':

Attitude

- Willingness to do the job and enthusiasm for what you do
- Proactivity, responsibility and reliability
- Confidence that you can do the job and the motivation to do it
- Empathy, emotional intelligence and the ability to build rapport

Skills

- Technical ability
- Relevant experience

- Problem solving and decision-making capability
- Management/leadership skills where appropriate

Knowledge

- Technical understanding of the role
- An appreciation for the company and what it does
- Appropriate academic capability for the role
- A capacity for continual learning

If you are shy or don't like blowing your own trumpet, remember that you are *helping them* to establish that you are the right person for the job.

You might also look at it from another perspective. In an interview, they are giving you the opportunity, indeed permission, to demonstrate your credibility and ability to connect.

To think about the company's values...83
To explore some interview questions about the job... 97
Or continue to interview preparation...

95. Interview Preparation

When you are invited to an interview, particularly to a new company, it can be useful to have a checklist of things to gather, consider and do. Whilst the ideas below may seem obvious, they are designed to give you greater confidence for the interview itself.

Starting with the practical logistics:

- Where are you meant to be going?
- What time do you need to be there?
- How long will it take to get there (including contingency time)?
- Who will you need to ask for when you arrive?
- Where can you park (if relevant) and do you need to book a space?
- What is the dress code?

What you need to take with you:

- What, if anything, have they asked you to bring?
- Take a professional folder containing your interview invitation, a map or directions, CV/Application, job details, blank paper and a few pens.

In terms of the things you need to consider, read and think about:

- What specific job are you going for? What is the job title? What is the level of responsibility of the job? Will you be managing other people?
- What information is available to you as the candidate, i.e. advert, job particulars etc.? Have you read these and made notes? Have you read the job description,

including the main objectives of the job and where the job fits within the organisation? Have you got some examples of where you meet the criteria of the job?

- Have you done a thorough check through their website?
- Are you aware of any sensitive or potentially challenging issues connected with the job... and how you might handle these when you are in post?

Start thinking about the interview process. Ask yourself:

- How do I want to come across?
- What do I need to get across?

To remind yourself why preparation is important... 14
To develop your organisational thinking... 82
Or continue to interview readiness...

96. *Interview Readiness*

Now, here is the most practical tip for interview preparation… and it is so obvious that *most people don't do it*!

Are you ready? Drum roll…!

Write down a list of questions that you might get asked in the interview!

These will be:

- Technical/operational (to do with your job expertise, knowledge and experience)
- Personal/interpersonal qualities/skills (to do with how you organise/conduct yourself and how you interact with others)
- Managerial (if relevant, i.e. how you manage/lead individuals/teams successfully and how you manage wellbeing and performance)

Then, use your current knowledge and your *Resource Pot* (see Piece 70) to help you in developing an answer, *with examples and evidence,* to each and every question. Remember what they are looking for: Can you and will you do the job… and how will you add value?

You will usually be invited to ask them a question or two at the end… and it is generally a good idea to ask *something*. A useful default question might be: "What learning & development opportunities are there within the role?"

You may have very specific questions you want to ask to clarify something about the role or help you make your decision. If not, here are some other questions you could ask:

- Can you tell me more about the team I would be joining (e.g. how long have they been together?)
- Can you tell me more about the culture of the company and what is important?
- What kind of social events take place?

When should you discuss salary? It is not uncommon for salary to be discussed *after* the first interview, but if they bring it up, be ready to answer. Is the salary stated up front, or is there a 'range' (from-to or between x and y)? If they ask you what salary you are looking for, you might base this on your previous experience levels. Avoid the lowest figure but be realistic. Demonstrate that you are happy to discuss this (i.e. negotiate), but remember you will be in a stronger position to negotiate *after* they have decided they want to offer you the job!

Be careful with the questions you ask as they could have unintended consequences. For example, if you ask about promotional opportunities, it may look as if you are proactive and ambitious… but it may also look like you are already looking for the next job.

To demonstrate how you stay resilient… 40
To explore how you handle motivation… 124
Or continue to questions about the job…

97. Questions About the Job

Here are some specific questions you might get asked. Remember, this is simply a starting point.

The organisation/department

- What attracts you to working here?
- What do you know about us as an organisation/ department?

The job you are applying for

- What in particular interests you about this job?
- What qualities do you think you can bring to the job and what areas (if any) do you think you will find challenging?
- What do you think the main purpose of this job is?

Your current or previous job

- Was there a particular job in your past that you especially enjoyed? Why?
- What new systems or procedures have you introduced in your previous work experience?
- What kind of decisions have you been expected to make in previous jobs?
- What is a typical day for you? Please describe.
- How do you plan your day?
- Have you ever been in a conflict situation at work? If so, how did you deal with it and how was it resolved?
- If you have a large volume of urgent work how would you cope with it? How would you prioritise?
- When you had to do a job that was particularly uninteresting, how did you deal with it?

- Describe a time in any job you have held when you were faced with problems or pressures which tested your ability to cope. What did you do? What did you learn from this?
- Why do you want to change jobs?

Remember to answer questions to the job you are applying for. If they ask you about the future, then you can tell them more about any aspirations you may have. However, they are looking for someone to fulfil a specific role, not necessarily someone who will want to move on in a short time period.

To show how you manage your time…64
To utilise your resource pot… 70
Or continue to questions about you…

98. Questions About You

As well as questions about the job itself, be prepared to answer questions about you, your skills, your qualities and how you handle situations, for example:

Teamwork

- What did you do in your last job to contribute towards teamwork? Be specific.
- Give me an example of a time when you feel you were able to motivate your colleagues?

Personality

- How would your best friend describe you?
- What makes you laugh?

Training

- What have you done over the past two years to develop yourself personally and professionally?
- What training (if any) would you need to undertake for this job?

Future Career

- What are your future aspirations?
- Where do you see yourself in e.g. 5 years' time?

Professional Skills

Be prepared to answer questions about (and hence come up with good examples of) the following key skills:

- Technical and IT,
- Planning, organising and prioritising,
- Problem solving,

- Decision making,
- Communicating,
- Influencing and negotiating,
- Team-working,
- Managing, delegating and allocating resources,
- Leading, coaching and motivating
- Resolving conflict.

Some questions may be in the form of case studies or 'what if...' situations. For example: "Tell me about a stressful situation you've faced... and how did you cope with that?" or "What if you were managing an individual who announced that they were feeling extremely stressed? How might you handle that?"

To talk about your key qualities... 74
To discuss how you might resolve conflicts... 117
Or continue to tough interview questions...

99. *Tough Interview Questions*

A tough question could be defined as any question you do not have an answer to! Difficult questions can put you on the spot... on the back foot... in the headlights... and you may find it useful to read Piece 77 to develop some strategies for handling questions when you don't have the answer to hand. However, here are two types of tough questions and ideas on how to handle them effectively.

1) Your greatest weakness?
A classic difficult question is based around asking you for your greatest strength (and this should be easy to answer) followed by your greatest weakness (which is less easy because it places you in a potential 'double-bind' – damned if you answer it honestly but damned if you answer is disingenuously or do not answer it at all). One method is to give a weakness that might also be a strength (e.g. "sometimes I'm a bit of a perfectionist"). However, an *even more* productive answer might be to give an example but say how you have overcome it. Put the weakness in the past and demonstrate that when you discover a weakness, you take action to deal with it. For example: "I used to get a bit too focussed on seeing a task through to completion, but now I've learnt to set it to one side and come back to it later if a higher priority task comes up."

Interviewers may ask this question to test your level of self-awareness (e.g. about your weaknesses) and also proactivity (in learning to improve yourself and resolve problems).

2) If you were a... what would you be and why?
Another strange question is the metaphor question. For example, if you were a type of animal or bird or kitchen

implement what would you be and why. The point of these questions is usually to test your spontaneity and creativity. If you have a good answer, then great… go for it! However, when under pressure in an interview, it can be hard to think on the spot. If you *cannot* think of an immediate answer, first pick a strength or strong quality you have. Then… what animal/bird/kitchen implement might have that quality?

If you still cannot think of e.g. a bird, then simply state the quality: "Hmmm, which bird would best demonstrate [strength]?" or "Well, it would have to be a bird that is able to organise themselves effectively [positive quality]. I'd have to think about that!" If you *still* cannot think of a metaphor, at least you have part answered the question (i.e. given the why).

Other challenging questions to consider

- If there is a gap in your working CV, be prepared to answer *what you did between jobs*. E.g. maternity/paternity leave, caring for someone, volunteering? Think about the key skill/learning from that time that will help you with the job.
- *Why are you leaving your current job/company?* However, you choose to answer this question, avoid criticising your previous manager/ employer… even if they were dreadful to you. Focus on the future and wanting to work in a company that reflects your values, where you can make a difference etc.
- *Do you not think you are overqualified for this job?* Do not make it sound as if this job is a stepping stone. Acknowledge your experience, tell them why you want to do this specific job.

To get better at using metaphor… 29
To think about why you want to change companies… 36
Or continue to interviews: on your best behaviour…

100. Interviews: On Your Best Behaviour

From the moment you make first contact to the point where you leave the site after your interview, act as if **all** the folks you meet are interviewing and evaluating you. For example:

- Members of the HR team, Security and Reception
- Whoever escorts you to and from the interview room
- Anyone you meet along the way (e.g. colleagues, assistants and cleaning, kitchen, restaurant/coffee shop staff). Indeed… anyone you speak to before, during or after the official interview!

For anyone you have contact with: make eye contact, smile, be kind, be friendly and speak confidently… You are endeavouring to make a good first impression, to build layers of connection and credibility, to be seen as likable, confident, competent, honest and trustworthy.

Just before you go in to the interview itself (i.e. as you are about to step into the interview room), develop the Confidence Stance (raise your sternum an inch and bring your head up). Then, as you see the interviewer(s), make eye contact and smile. Shake hands only with people who offer it. If they do not tell you where to sit (or make it obvious), then ask them: "Where would you like me to sit?" A good general tip is: 'ask before you act'.

And just for fun, here are some things to avoid doing (all of which I have seen or heard about actually happening!):

- Avoid making negative or sarcastic comments about the company or their venue. I once heard about an interviewee who complained, during the interview, that the clock on the wall was too loud!

- Avoid complaining… about the journey, the parking, the location, the people you have met so far, the toilets, the room you are in. Simply put, no matter how much you would like to give them feedback… avoid complaining!
- Avoid tutting, rolling your eyes, making inappropriate jokes, swearing, talking to only one person in the room (if there is a team of interviewers), playing with your phone, texting, taking a call, crying, smelling of alcohol or body odour… you get the idea!
- Do not take shopping bags or suitcases into the interview room. The exception is a smart handbag or satchel.
- This last one is going to sound really pedantic, but consider the impressions! Avoid, wherever possible, taking a coat into the interview. Leave it in the car or at reception if you are able. Only take a coat if it is *absolutely* necessary (e.g. freezing cold/pouring rain).
    - If you wear a coat *into* the interview, it will look as if you are ready to leave again (especially if you leave it on). If you take it off in the room, then the first memory they have of you will be disrobing.
    - If you *have* to take a coat in, carry it smartly and after making eye contact, smiling and greeting, ask where you can put your coat (or ask if you can put it on a coat rack or chair).
    - Do not put your jacket on the back of the chair without asking – it can make you look arrogant!

To think about what creates the wrong impression… 72
To focus on your confidence… 76
Or continue to networking: why and wherefore…

101. Networking: Why and Wherefore

No matter whether you are employed or self-employed, networking is an essential way of keeping in touch with your professional marketplace and up-to-date with current thinking.

If you are self-employed, networking may be one of your gateways to new and continued work. If you are employed, networking will help you maintain your profile, strengthen your connections and give you a sense of what is happening outside your company.

Within the networking skillset, we might say there are three key roles[i]. Although individuals will usually be better at some things than others, you may want to look at developing all three:

1. **Collector:** The expert, the learner and sharer of knowledge. They are the innovator… the ideas person. They gather information and help others to solve problems. Strong collectors are seen as highly credible and trustworthy (in their field).
2. **Connector**: The person with many others in their network. Strong connectors also get to know their connections personally and/or professionally. They are good at establishing what others do/offer and what they need. They are good at putting folks in contact with each other, acting as a hub. They know 'people who know people' and are keen to connect you with others.
3. **Convincer:** Able to make the case and get people to buy-in. They can move their audience emotionally and are

good at forging agreements. They tend to be good negotiators, influencers and sales reps.

If you are only strong in one area, you might have great ideas but no way of getting them across. Or you might have a lovely network of people who like you and think you are great, but you might not be getting your own message across. Alternatively, you might be a great salesperson but with nothing to sell!

So, consider how you might integrate all three areas:

- Get out there and build your network.
- Recommend other people and put them in contact with each other.
- Seek connections and 'overlaps' with others. No-one needs to be your competitor! You may do similar things but you may also add value to one another. What innovations might you create with someone?
- Be prepared to share ideas and help people solve their own problems. Get known as a go-to person, a fixer, an expert in your field.
- Consider what you have to offer and how it might be valuable to others. Ask questions about what they do, what their challenges are and what they need.
- Stay kind, friendly, upbeat, warm and welcoming.
- Support and refer others whilst letting them know what *you* do too.

To reflect further as to why networking is essential... 73
To build your online network... 105
Or continue to make networking easier...

102. Make Networking Easier

If you find networking uncomfortable, you are not alone. At every event, there are likely to be lots of attendees who are shy, introverted and do not delight in talking to strangers! Whether you are confident or less so, when you are networking, make it *easy* for yourself with these steps…

1) Prepare. If you find that conversations can be a bit awkward, then have a set of questions you can ask each person you meet, for example: What do you do? Who do you work for? How are you finding the event? Are you looking for anything particular in coming to this event? How long have you been a member? Have you been to these events before? How can I help you? (Some of these questions will depend on what kind of event you are attending and also where the conversation takes you).
2) If there is a list of delegates available before the event, have a look and see if there is anyone you would like to meet. Perhaps you might check a few of them on social media. At some point during the event, ask the organisers if they can point that person out or introduce you.
3) When you first get there and have 'booked in', walk confidently to the coffee point. Get a drink – turn around and survey the scene! You might even meet someone at the coffee point to get you started!
4) If someone is on their own, you could talk to them.
5) If 'interrupting' a pair, ask: "may I join you?" Most people will be happy with that (perhaps relieved) but don't take it personally if they are having a private conversation.
6) Ask them questions about what they do. Be clear about what you do but avoid overselling.

7) Swap business cards, say you will connect with them online and do so later.
8) Stay in touch with interesting connections!
9) Have an 'exit' line to move on politely. Say something like: "It's been good talking with you. Enjoy the rest of the event", "I'll catch up with you later", "There's someone I need to catch up with" or "Time to mingle!"

If you are looking for a regular networking organisation, be aware that not all groups are equal! Some are 'clique', some are morguelike(!) and some are chatty, friendly and welcoming. Find the ones that suit you!

When you have a business purpose for networking, get clear about your message (e.g. why you are going, who you are, what do you deliver, who are you looking for, who do you want to talk to, what do you have in common with others, what questions could you ask, what services might you need?)

And finally, the biggest secret for making it easy? Keep going! Become part of the community. Attend regularly and you will begin to get to know people. After a few visits, you may then establish a set of 'friends'. Today's strangers are next week's friendly faces!

To reflect on what builds rapport... 56
To develop your brand awareness... 71
Or continue to networking presence and panache...

103. Networking Presence and Panache!

There is sometimes a fine line between appearing totally confident versus arrogant and cocky. The trick is to be comfortable in your own boots with a degree of humility.

Think of those folks you know who have positive presence in a group environment. Most of them will be friendly, visible, smiling, kind, welcoming and have a strong voice (audible when chatting to them in a crowded room). They ask questions and seem genuinely interested in others. They are also interesting and engaging. They are clear about who they are and what they do, but they don't come across as pushy or desperate to sell. They will often be on a committee or act as a representative/ambassador. But even when they are not part of the committee, they act like an informal host. They help to connect you with other people and may even introduce you if they think you and they have something in common.

So, if you have been to the group before, be welcoming to the new attendees. If it is their first time there, they will tend to assign credibility and authority to you… and will often start asking you about the networking session/group as if you are an expert!

We are focussing here on constructive behaviours that build a positive reputation. Although it should go without saying, there is a set of behaviours to avoid (and I have seen networkers do all of these): swearing, 'dissing' other companies/ competitors/organisers, getting really angry about politics/ex-wife etc, disrespecting/interrupting/talking over other networkers!

What can you do if you encounter bad behaviour in others? If someone is seemingly rude, disinterested or condescending, they may be nervous or shy… or they may be the type of person you are best off avoiding! There are some who may lose interest in you if they think you are not useful in some way (best avoided… they may be a 'player'). If you find a lot of people like that, you may need to question if this is the right networking group for you.

In terms of making the best of the networking group, here are some final suggestions:

- Make friends with the organisers.
- If you use some else's services and are happy with the service, publicise the fact. Promote and praise them verbally, online and in print. It will also put you in a good light.
- Contribute to the group publication (if there is one).
- Be a speaker/presenter (if possible and if relevant).
- Put useful articles on the group's social media.
- If possible (and if time allows), offer to join or support the committee.
- Ask in what other ways you might contribute.
- The more you add value to the group, the more you will feel part of the community and the more likely you will find the group useful and engaging.

To develop your natural confidence… 28
To deal with difficult behaviours in others… 116
Or continue to what's in a name…

104. What's in a Name?

How do you introduce yourself?
How do you say your name?

Seems simple enough, doesn't it? You have been doing it for years! However, is it having the impact you desire?

Firstly, the order of the words (particularly if you are giving your first and last name). Consider the following:

1. Hello, I'm James Bond.
2. My name's James Bond.
3. My name's James. James Bond.
4. The name's Bond. James Bond.

Most people, in my experience, go with the first option and it is probably the most obvious when introducing yourself to a group of peers. The second option is, perhaps, a little more formal and credible. However, if I am (for example) introducing myself at the start of a presentation, I tend to use the third option. It is functional, slightly different but gets my first name out there twice. It is important to pause a little, otherwise listeners might think I was called Joe-Joe Cheal. The fourth option is, of course, useful if you are James Bond!

Secondly, your intonation… where do you put the emphasis and where do you 'rise and fall' in your pitch? The advice around credibility is: go up at the start and down at end (for gravity). If you go up at the end, it can sound like a question! Try it out for yourself now, make it subtle… and notice the difference.

Some folk seem a little apologetic when saying their name, both in tonality and facial expressions. It is as if they are expecting a negative reaction. Of course, many people get teased about their name (especially at school). I had various nick-names: 'Cheese' and 'Lemon Peel' spring to mind (which now looks like the ingredients for a rather delicious dessert!) I have also noticed that some parents seem to be quite ignorant (or cruel) when naming their children.

Be proud of your name. Research it. What is the etymology (i.e. where does the name come from and what does it mean)? If you don't like your name or feel it holds you back/does not give the best impression, remember that your name is your choice. I know a couple who, when they got married, chose a new last-name that they both felt more in tune with.

If your name is difficult for other cultures to pronounce, remember: there are certain sounds that different nationalities struggle with (as it is not in their learnt 'vocabulary'). I consider myself pretty good at making different sounds(!), but there are some I cannot get right. Be tolerant of others, especially if they do their best. Alternatively, make it part of your introduction to help others pronounce your name well. If done in a kind and friendly way, it can make a positive impression and make you memorable for the right reasons.

How do you want people to feel about you when they hear your name? What associations do you want them to make?

To remind yourself about credibility… 6
To influence how others remember you… 74
Or continue to build your online network…

105. Build Your Online Network

Online networking… what is the point of it? Beyond the wonderment of how many folks are out there doing similar things to you… it can be useful for establishing who people are in a company and hence give you the name of the right person. It can also be a useful sense check of what is happening 'out there' (and sometimes you can find all sorts of useful resources).

When used well, a professional online network is like a virtual CV/Profile, newsfeed and business card. It can tell others who you are, what you do and what you have done. It is an opportunity to build connection and credibility with the 'outside world'. You can build your network with folks who could be useful and who you could be useful to.

However, be prepared for many individuals not to respond to your invitation, messages or news. They may not necessarily be ignoring you; they may simply not be all that active on the network. And don't get your hopes up that others will immediately buy you or your services. It might happen but the probability is low!

In terms of inviting others to join your network, different folks appear to have different strategies as to whether they accept invitations:

1. Accept anyone.
2. Check the inviter – why do they want to connect?
3. Focus on 'quality' of connections, connecting only with those they have met or who are of genuine interest.

4. Despite setting up a profile, some hardly ever go on the network as they don't see the point (or don't have a need). Perhaps they don't bother because the only people trying to connect with them are also trying to sell them something…

Some folks are quite brutal in how they market themselves. They play a numbers game. Invite everybody and anybody to the maximum they are allowed. They post pictures and items out every day, gradually building a following. This is not my preferred style, but I guess it works for some.

If you want to invite someone, the best practice is to:

- Ask yourself: What are you trying to achieve? For example: to progress, to get in to a company, to create partnerships, to learn more about your industry (or theirs)? Who are the 'right people'?
- Look at the person's profile. Are they really the right person?
- Invite them with a message. Why are you looking to connect? What is your common ground/interest? Where did you meet them or how did you hear about them?

In terms of building your online network, actively invite those who (a) you have met and (b) are in the same field/groups (online and real world) as you… then seek to stay in contact with your high-quality connections. This way, you have your own version of 'circles' or layers of contacts, from your 'inner-circle' to the 'who-knows-one-day-might-be-helpful'.

To reflect on your role in how lucky you are… 12
To connect with the 'right people'… 89
Or continue to interacting online…

106. Interacting Online

You can use an online network as a passive online CV or you become more active, sharing thoughts, questions, articles and successes. It can help you to build credibility, even when your connections are not apparently engaging with you. I sometimes get folk who have never interacted with me online say: "Oh I see you've just written another book." So, the profile is getting out there subtly!

When seeking to message and interact with others, remember that there are different personality styles out there. Some will chat, interact and be helpful… and some will not! If you invite and connect with someone who you have not yet met, as a next step, you could ask for advice with an easy to answer question (that seems tailored to them rather than a generic question that looks like a lure).

Be smart about who you are 'selling to' and how you are selling. I get people trying to sell me leadership courses when this is what I have been doing for over 25 years! Or telling me that they can help me get a six-figure salary for my coaching business… there are plenty of scammers out there who will happily take your money… and you do *not* want to look like one of them!

If you are posting information, you can often get a sense of what is 'landing' and having an impact by the number of likes and views your posts get. As an example, here are the types of post that got the higher views/interaction for me over a six-month period. Most of these included a picture:

- Winning or being a finalist for an award.
- A clever idea or model that is timely to the current news/mood.
- Getting a book published, sharing a chapter download.
- Speaking at an event, thanking the host for inviting you to present.
- Attending something worthwhile (e.g. Mental Health course), including a picture with a colleague from another company.
- Visiting your old school!
- A genuine question e.g. clarification about a government policy that affects your role/field.
- Sharing a post from an influencer.
- Asking for help for someone else (e.g. a request or question from a charity you support).
- Updating your profile picture.
- A picture of a newspaper cutting with something you have achieved.

Of course, articles/blogs and videos can help to build credibility and connection too, particularly if 'framed' well. The words you use to *describe* the video or article need to be influential enough to pull people into taking an *active role* in reading/watching. Of course, video subtitles help!

To consider what and how much you might share… 51
To think about your brand awareness… 71
Or continue to dissolving dilemmas…

The Sixth Bit

Pieces About Challenges

107. How to Dissolve Career and Life Dilemmas

Often in life and work, we face a dilemma. Should I do this or that? Should I go this way or that way? Should I stay or should I go now? Should I be employed or self-employed? Change location/move house or stay where I am? Go for house 'a' or house 'b'?

Most management manuals will tell you to draw up a list of pros and cons, to do a forcefield analysis or use a range of decision-making tools. And this may work for you. However, to make a decision means to 'cut off' or 'strike off' one of the options. This might mean missing out on the advantages of the losing side.

Another approach is to see if there is a 'best of both worlds' solution; this means using 'both-and' thinking rather than 'either/or'. To do this, I developed a simple tool called the **Dilemma Integration Technique[i].**

Take a blank piece of paper and write the advantages of option 'a' randomly around on the page. Then write the advantages of option 'b' randomly around on the same page with the same pen, mixing it up so that all the collective advantages are interspersed. Now what you have is a jumbled list of what you actually want. If it helps, you could prioritise this list (into order of importance) or put scores (e.g. 1=less important, 5=more important). However, what you now have is a single list of criteria for a solution. What ideas does this spark in you? How might you achieve/gain/get all of the significant advantages?

The ability to think in 'both-and' terms is known as dialectic thinking and is the root to dissolving many dilemmas and resolving many conflicts. We are setting the foundation for innovation and for 'win/win' outcomes.

An Example...

Using the dilemma of 'change career or stay where I am', let us say that someone writes down the personal advantages of both sides (which may be different for you in your own context):

Variety Re-invigoration
Independence Teamworking
Friendships Security
Good atmosphere
Creative Problem Solving
New Challenges Easy Journey

How might this person get the best of their amalgamated criteria? Could they stay where they are *and* change their career? Might there be other opportunities in the same company they work for?

To develop skills in handling conflict... 117
To discover how to handle uncertainty... 122
Or continue to work-life balance...

108. Effects of Success on Work-Life Balance

There is a mindset (in many people) that to be successful in your career you have to give up your work-life balance. And sadly, some companies still perpetuate this mindset by rewarding and promoting those that 'put the hours in' and show dedication. However, things are changing. This '*sell your soul to the company store*' approach has been recognised as discriminatory and counter-productive to mental health and wellbeing.

This mindset is also known as the 'paradox of success'[i], i.e. you can have career success or a good home-life, but not both. This is, however, a limited 'either/or' perspective... a false choice (also known as a double-bind... damned of you do and damned if you don't!)

To get out of this apparent double-bind, we need to ask a couple of smart questions:

1. What is required to for me progress at work?
2. What is required for me to have a happy life?

The answer to the first question (aside from *read this book*!) is, in big picture terms: to deliver on what you have agreed to do, demonstrate confidence and competence and make sure the right people are aware of you.

The answer to the second question will be personal to you. What gives you a sense of wellbeing? What will you one day look back on and be glad you did? Who do you want to spend quality time with... and doing what? What do you want to discover, explore and learn about?

Now generalise success to meeting the answers to *both* of the questions above. It does not have to be an either/or!

You might also ask:

1. What do I get by having the best career?
2. What do I get by having the best home-life?

It is **your choice** to create and nurture a rewarding and stimulating career (*which may give you e.g. a sense of satisfaction and achievement, that you are making a difference*) whilst also developing and maintaining a great home-life and set of relationships (*which might give you e.g. a sense of wellbeing, happiness and achievement… that you are making a difference!*) This is another example of 'both-and' thinking.

When you are genuinely happy, confident and feel supported at home, you are more likely to feel happy, confident and supported at work… and vice versa. It *can* be a virtuous circle!

Success will depend on how you define and measure it. It will also depend on what standard (and who) are you gauging it by. Life itself is rarely perfect… and if you are comparing yourself to others, remember that their lives may not necessarily be as perfect as they appear (e.g. on social media).

To reconnect with your purpose… 32
To remind yourself about your choices… 45
Or continue to being prepared for success…

109. Being Prepared for Success

1) Lonely at the top?

One of the things I hear from people who have been promoted is that they suddenly feel unsupported by the next level up. They are alone and left to their own devices... unsure if they are doing the right things. This is not uncommon, particularly in large multinational organisations where senior management may be based in another country. It is not that they are bad managers, they are simply not as accessible. And you will be expected to 'step up'.

If you are looking to progress, get an understanding of the next role up as part of your preparation. If possible, do some job shadowing and ask the person in that position about the challenges as well as the details of the role itself[i].

2) Unsupportive manager?

At some point in your career, you may experience a genuinely unsupportive manager. You might have to face mixed messages & broken promises. You might be told that you are in the driving seat when really you are not (e.g. you have the illusion of control... responsibility without authority). You might also have a manager who tells you that if you keep going, you will be good enough to progress... and then it is always "probably next year".

Sometimes, you will need to take control of your next steps and work with and around your manager. Do not expect them to make your next career move happen. Make sure it is in your hands.

3) Expect criticism and envy!

You might never have to face it, but as you become more and more successful, you may experience flashes of envy and jealousy towards you: e.g. "you're lucky", "it's alright for you", "who did you have to kiss up to?", "it's not fair, I deserved that job" etc. The more you step up, the more some individuals may see you as fair game for criticism.

Be impeccable! Treat others kindly, be humble and know that you have got to where you are because (a) you have put the effort in and (b) other people have seen the potential in you. Take criticism as feedback data and decide if you need to take action. Treat it as a sign that you are being successful!

To explore the benefits of mentoring... 90
To deal with a lack of direction from above... 123
Or continue to not enough time...

110. Not Enough Time

A classic reason I hear for *not* focussing on career and living goals is that 'there is not enough time'. Oh dear! The reality here is that time exists… but priorities are our choice. When someone says: "I don't have time to do that" what they are really saying is "I don't see that as a priority".

Sometimes, we have so much to do that we only have time to work on our growing to-do list. No time to delegate or train others. No time to network or build connections.

Here are some general rules:

- Negotiate and then prioritise your objectives and hence your to do list.
- Make 'breaks' (i.e. coffee area networking opportunities) a priority. Get away from your desk. You need breaks anyway to perform properly.
- Manage expectations on an ongoing basis about what you are going to be able to deliver and by when.
- Look at who you could delegate to and train them whilst you are doing the task.

If lack of time really has become a problem, or rather the 'to-do' list has become a monster, here are some tips to get back on top of things[i]:

- Check out your Re%Pro (see Piece 64). If the problem is high reactivity, write down all the reactive tasks that affect your time (and all the things that make you reactive). Do some problem solving to reduce/eliminate some of the reactivity.

- Get more realistic about how long things will take. They will usually take longer than you think (in part because of all the reactive interruptions).
- If your to-do list has become overwhelming, treat this as a '*master* to-do' list. At the start of each day or week draw a few things down from the '*master* to-list' into an '***active*** to-do list' and then focus on those few things. If you need to pull something down, then push something else back up... and *that* will be the thing you might not get done today!
- Look at the items on your to-do list and decide which of them will give you the best short- and long-term gains. Act on those that will add most value.

To ready yourself for opportunities... 13
To reconnect to what is important... 31
Or continue to dealing with pressure...

111. Dealing with Pressure

Pressure is part of everyday work. Some pressures you can alleviate or remove, but some pressures will remain and will have to be 'lived with'. When helping people deal with pressure, I use the three stages of 'cause >> filter >> effect':

Cause >>	Filter >>	Effect
<u>**Pressure**</u> The demand put on you (by yourself or others).	<u>**Perception**</u> How you see/frame it and what meaning you give it.	<u>**Stress**</u> The symptoms, how you feel (physical, emotional, mental).
Change/influence the situation if possible. Or adapt and accept. (It is what it is!)	*Change the internal experience (interpretations, perspective, states).*	*Look after yourself. Take some 'you' time to recharge your batteries.*

Pressure is the cause… stress is the effect and the filter will affect *how* you perceive the pressure and hence whether it becomes stress. Did you know that there is a positive version of stress called 'eustress'?

The idea here is that we have three approaches to tackling pressure if it becomes an issue. You may not be able to do **all** of these for a given situation, but you could do some:

1) Alleviating the pressure:
   - Remove the cause (drop it)
   - Organise yourself (get back in control)
   - Communicate assertively (say 'no'/'not now', be clear about your boundaries – what is possible within a given timescale, update others about what is/not going to be delivered)

- Learn (develop new skills and knowledge)
- Problem solve (get an outcome and a plan to resolve the pressure point)

2) Manage your perception:
    - How important is it really (e.g. will it matter in 10 years' time)?
    - Reframe it (what could be good about this/useful here? Seek opportunities)
    - Step back (write it down, get some distance on it)
    - Have I experienced this before? How did I handle it then?
    - Whatever happens, I can handle it![i]

3) Look after yourself:
    - What can you do *during* the day and at the *end* of the day to 'unwind'?
    - How does stress and tension hit you? Physically (e.g. aches, pains and tiredness)? Emotionally (e.g. irritable, getting cross, tears)? Mentally (e.g. cannot think/focus, cloudy head)? Notice the early warning signs!
    - Choose to 'MAKE' time rather than 'find' time to relax in some way. Do things that 'soften' you physically, mentally and emotionally… dissolve that tension.
    - Aside from all the 'roles' you play out (e.g. parent, partner, manager, team member) when do you take time to simply be 'you'? Make time for yourself.

To generate ideas for dealing with pressure… 49
To make sure you are being realistic about time… 64
Or continue to working from home…

112. Working from Home

Some folks love working from home and some really struggle; they might need help in 'switching on/off' at the start and end of the day or they may be feeling alone and isolated because they are not with others in the office.

1) Switching on/off

I recently heard the question: am I working from home or living at work? It is essential to find a way of separating work-life from home-life… even if you love your job!

The idea of separating work from home is to create a psychological gap, a way of telling the brain 'work is done – this is home time' and vice versa. I have seen this described as an 'airlock'.

At the end of the working day, you could:

- Update your to-do list with things that are still outstanding. This helps put work to bed and means you don't need to remember it all overnight.
- Switch off laptop/devices. Hear the click of the closing laptop… and relax!
- Close the door to the work area.
- If working in a living area, put everything away (laptop/paperwork/work-phone into a box).
- Avoid getting sucked back into work because someone in your team (or your manager) is working different hours to you. Let others know your core hours (e.g. at the bottom of your emails). Or switch on the 'out of office' message on your email.
- Get changed. Or at the very least, change your shoes.

- Go for a quick drive (if that allows you to relax)! Some people go and simply sit in their car for a few minutes, listening to the radio.
- I know one chap who would go out of his front door in the morning, walk round the house and re-enter the house via the back door. He would then go into his office. At the end of the day, he did the reverse!

What else do you do at the end (or start) of the working day to tell your brain that it is time to focus on something else?

2) Feeling engaged with others

For some, it is not so much the switching off, but the feeling of isolation from their colleagues. For these folks, it is the social aspect that they miss[i]. If this describes you, you are not alone!

Check out who else in the team would like to catch up. Have virtual coffee/lunchtime breaks. Rather than using task-oriented team-meetings as a place to see how others are doing, make a point of setting up socials. Some teams do online quizzes and other creative things to have fun. Remember that some folk in the team may not really want to play!

Find like-minded colleagues and catch up on a one-to-one basis. Stay in touch with those who feel the same way.

To make the best of video-conferencing… 85
To handle a lack of direction from others… 123
Or continue to not sleeping well…

113. Not Sleeping Well?

Sleep is such an essential and lovely thing (as far as I am concerned!) It does seem that different people function and thrive on different amounts of sleep, however, we all need quality rest.

Insomnia can hit us at different times. If you cannot get to sleep in the first place or are waking up in the middle of the night (or early morning) and cannot get back to sleep then you might try some of the ideas below to discover what works best for you:

1) Before going to bed (or early evening)

- Eat your evening meal earlier (e.g. 6.00 pm) and avoid heavy snacks. Limit alcohol (i.e. not every night!)
- Avoid caffeine later in the day (I have about 1.00pm as my cut off point).
- Do some relaxation exercises (e.g. meditation).
- Have a bath (very good for relaxing and managing depression). Or have a shower – wash away the troubles of the day.
- Write down the best thing that happened today (e.g. in a journal/diary).
- Read something easy, relaxing and distracting.

2) During the night

- If you have thoughts buzzing in your head, keep a notepad, pen and nightlight by your bed to write ideas, worries and concerns down. Keep them top level and minimal.
- Get up and do something quiet e.g. reading[i].
- Listen to audio (e.g. quiet music or books) with comfortable earphones. I have recordings of things I

watched as a child (e.g. The Wombles, Mr Men, Magic Roundabout) because my brain still associates them with relaxing and pleasure. Plus, they are very easy listening. It helps distract me from thinking and hence I tend to fall asleep again.

- Use relaxation techniques. Explore approaches that help you to quieten your mind and turn down the internal chatter or worrier.
- Troubled with nightmares? Write the nightmare down and then rewrite it from where it went 'wrong' and change the ending so that it has a more positive and empowering outcome.

3) General

- Make sure the heating is off. Have the window open or closed (depending on your preference).
- Keep unnatural lights out (e.g. computers, digital clocks)
- No pets on the bed, either when you are trying to sleep or at other times. Many people have slight allergies to pet hair/fur which can affect sleep.
- Change your bedding regularly (to prevent mild allergies). And if it has been a while, you might consider a new mattress.

To explore some ways to retrain your brain... 41
To find ways to deal with your 'internal worrier'... 48
Or continue to career blockers and traps...

114. 'No Opportunities' and 'No Experience' Traps

Within the potholes and pitfalls of promotion and progression there are a couple of classic career blockers… no opportunities available and not enough experience. If we cannot see the opportunities and we are not in a state of readiness, it will be tougher to 'get lucky'. So, here are some ideas…

1) Creating opportunities where there are none

For many people, the reason why there appears to be no opportunities is because they are setting their sights to narrow. If someone wants their manager's job (and they then rule out all other possibilities), they will have to wait for their manager to move on. If their manager likes their job, this could be a long wait!

If there are genuinely no other opportunities in the company you work for, ask yourself: "What do I enjoy now and what would I get from progressing?" Write down the answers. Can you find these things in your organisation in other ways? If you like the company you work for, it may be worth exhausting the possibilities there first before taking the decision to leave. Can you develop your role with higher-level responsibility for example?

If you want a specific role (e.g. your manager's job), ask yourself: "What is it about that role that appeals to me? What would doing that role give me?" Again, are there ways of developing your readiness? Can you gain some experience by getting your manager to delegate to you? Can you do some job shadowing? Can you join them in certain meetings as an observer? What can you do to develop some of the 'next level' skills? Are there other roles that would give you what you really want?

2) Gaining experience when there is none to be had.

There is a circular 'catch 22' paradox *(known as the 'permission paradox')* that some people face when it comes to gaining enough experience to be considered for a role… You cannot get the job due to lack of experience… but you cannot get the experience due to not having done that job! So how else can you gain experience? As above, can you take on some tasks from your manager or get some mentoring?

In terms of making your CV more robust, you could:

- Highlight relevant experience/skills/qualifications from other jobs you have done… the transferable skills.
- Talk to those who have recently got into the industry/role that you would like to get into. Ask them what they did to get the role and how did they get started?
- Seek out some volunteering roles that will help you develop the right experience.
- If you are really keen (and can afford to do it), you might look at an apprenticeship/internship.

To discover how self-disclosure could help you… 51
To explore how to get a salary increase… 61
Or continue to "it's not me"…

115. It's Not Me... (Oh Dear! Maybe It Is Me!)

Self-awareness is a truly marvellous thing! It is all too easy to leave a job and blame your old manager or the organisation for your disgruntlement. Of course, you may have been unlucky (or chosen unluckily). You may indeed have had a terrible manager and the company you worked for may have genuinely been unethical and unkind. However, if you have left two or three jobs in just a few years, whether it was because of the company, the management or colleagues you didn't like, then check if there are any patterns. What if (and I say this only hypothetically) the common denominator is you?

This is not to make you or anyone else the 'guilty party'. This is not about self-recrimination or deprecation. It is more about you enjoying your next role. If someone has a pattern running, there is a risk of them taking their 'stuff' from one job to another. They might have experienced and left a number of toxic environments, but surely it would be a tragedy to take the toxicity with them? Some people have expectations so high they are simply fantasy. Sadly, there is no *perfect* organisation!

Whilst this may be the territory of more intense personal development, here are a couple of things that might help someone raise their level of self-awareness. And since this also applies to relationship patterns, it could be a next step to a happier and more fulfilling life!

1) Family of origin?

There is a therapeutic/group dynamics concept called 'family of origin'[i]. What if, when we enter a new group, we replay our family scripts (usually from childhood). Perhaps colleagues become siblings (with rivalries and factions) and managers become parents. What if we inadvertently project our old role models/ archetypes onto the folks we currently work with? It is an interesting thought, is it not?

If this somehow rings true for you, then part of the letting go of toxicity is to keep reminding yourself that these new people are not your old family. Seek what is different about the new people in comparison to your family of origin.

2) Generalised beliefs

As human beings, we build generalisations about the world in order to survive. These generalisations are a type of belief (i.e. this is the way the world is and this is the way the world *should* be). You could have beliefs and bias about business in general, the sector you are in, the company you work for, leadership, managers, work colleagues and folks you manage! If you want to uncover some of your 'not-so-positive' beliefs write a list for each of the following (be honest!):

- The problem with the company I work for is…
- The problem with management is…
- The problem with work is…
- The problem with some colleagues is…

Then write down the exceptions to what you have written and when each of the above is actually rather good…

To explore limiting beliefs… 37
To seek feedback… 50
Or continue to dealing with difficult behaviours…

116. Dealing with Difficult Behaviours

There will be times during your career and life where you may face a person who is challenging to be around. Of course, we, ourselves, can all be a 'difficult person'! There are plenty of books on 'how to deal with difficult people' for further study. However, here are a few thoughts to get you started.

1) **The worst kind of difficult:** Be safe. If you feel that someone is a threat, make sure that you are protected (physically, financially, emotionally etc.) If you feel genuinely uncomfortable with an individual, be prepared to leave the room… 'In doubt? Get out!' Even when not actually threatening, there are some individuals we simply will not win over. Although relatively rare, there are psychopaths and sociopaths in the workplace[i] and in the neighbourhood. If there is nothing else you can do about them, then there is no shame in packing up and heading somewhere else.

2) **The tantrum:** When a person acts out, hurl insults etc, particularly if it all feels over the top and unwarranted:
    - Think of them as a child acting out. You might say: "You seem really angry about something… what's happened?" and then: "What do you need?"
    - Remember that it is not really your face they are seeing. They may be mapping historical internal representations onto you[ii]. It is not about you, but perhaps what you represent at that moment.
    - Be prepared to apologise for anything you may have actually done wrong though!

3) **The irritator:** Some people we find difficult in the sense that they annoy us or 'push our buttons'.
    - Are they really difficult or just different to you? Do they do or say things in different ways to how you think others should behave? It might be a difference in personality style, culture or language. Beware of your own 'unconscious bias'. The answer to this one is to broaden your tolerance... a personal development journey!
    - Separate the person from the behaviour. You can get to like a person, even if you don't enjoy everything they do or say. That is called a relationship!
    - If possible, develop some empathy for them by discovering *what has happened to cause them to behave that way*. Empathy dissolves anger. Consider: what if *a difficult person is a person in difficulty*? You are more likely to want to help a person in difficulty than a difficult person... but what if they are one and the same thing.

To explore bias and it's affects... 38
To find ways to build rapport... 56
Or continue to how to handle conflict...

117. How to Handle Conflict

The first step in handling a conflict… is wanting to handle the conflict! It takes psychological and emotional effort to resolve an issue between two people, especially if we are one of them.

There is a mindset that goes along with conflict resolution, a *'both-and' approach* where both parties get what they need from the situation. In addition, what does the conflict/problem itself need? If we find a way forward that meets our needs but does not meet the need of the problem itself… it will almost certainly resurface.

Be an 'integrator'… if you have a conflict (or simply a difference) of ideas/proposals/plans/solutions, then in order to find a way forward, *stop arguing or telling the other person why their idea will not work*! Instead:

1) ask them to tell you more about their approach. Listen carefully.
2) Tell them what you like about their idea (i.e. the benefits to the organisation): "What I like about your idea is that it gives us X,Y,Z."
3) Then say: "My approach is to… and that would give us A,B,C."
4) Now, is there a third way we could explore, a best of both worlds solution that would give us ABCXYZ?

For a general approach to 'stuck-ness' (particularly if there is an emotive, values clash element or there is a 'history' to it)[i]:

1) Start with the bigger picture, common ground (e.g. "I think we both want the project to succeed.")

2) Acknowledge their position: "I get that X is important to you."
3) Ask for more information: "Tell me more about what's happened/what the situation is from your perspective."
4) Ask what they need: "and so what do you need from me or from the situation?" Write it down.
5) Explain your side: "What's happening from my perspective is…" (avoid blame).
6) State what you need: "and what I need from you/this situation is…" Write it down.
7) Now look for joint solutions with the other party, something that meets the main needs of both sides and can be agreed and acted upon.

Easy? Not necessarily, but it is a start… and it sets the foundation for a more constructive conversation.

As an aside, if you are stuck in a conversation where the other person is not happy and you are not sure what to say or do, the question: "What do you need (from me)?" (or "What do you need (from me) right now?") can be a useful 'rescue question'. It stops you from trying to 'solve a problem' but keeps the dialogue going.

To explore ways to close the gap… 55
To find out what is important to the other party… 59
Or continue to dealing with resistance…

118. Dealing with Resistance

You might propose an idea or be involved in making change happen. Inevitably, there will be some folk who are not happy, do not want things to change or they want to do something else. In effect, they do *not* want to agree, buy-in, get on board etc.

The first tip in *preventing* resistance is to involve the other party in the decision making/problem solving/outcome setting/ planning/delivery. This way, they don't feel the whole thing has been imposed upon them. In addition, people do *not* tend to reject their own ideas.

The second tip, if you are in a group environment, is to write the resistance down (e.g. concerns, questions, objections). If you have access to a flip-chart then use that. If not make a point of writing the issues down on a notepad. Repeat them back/summarise them as necessary, and then address the concerns one-by-one in the order you want to handle them. This way, you are staying on control of a potentially fiery situation.

The third tip is a mind-bender! A moment of zen, as it were...

What if there is no such thing as resistance,
but simply attraction to an alternative?

If you imagine a person as resistant, how do you picture them? Try it with a person you know. Imagine them. How do they look? Arms folded? Grumpy, stern or disapproving face? Now imagine the same person as being attracted to an alternative. How does that change your imagined picture of them? For me, I imagine them looking in another direction (rather than at me), but they are happy with or interested in the thing that they are facing/looking at.

If the other person/party is attracted to an alternative, this generates some useful questions:

- What are they attracted to?
- What is it that makes the alternative so attractive to them?
- What are they gaining there that they don't think they will get from your proposal?

Even if their attraction is 'things staying the same', by looking at that 'thing' from their perspective, we can identify the benefits to them of that 'thing'. This leads us to the next step:

- How can I incorporate and demonstrate those benefits in my proposal or the change?
- How will they gain those benefits?

In this way, we are using the other party's resistance to inform our own proposal. For example, if they believe that the alternative approach gives them a sense of safety, show them how your idea is safe too. By building the alternative 'attractors' into the new way of doing things, the other party then has less reason to be resistant.

To improve your ability to make your case... 60
To be the positive force for change... 87
Or continue to making the best of change...

119. Making the Best of Change

Change is inevitable and constant. We cannot stand still for very long. Look at what happens to organisations that cannot adapt to the marketplace quickly or effectively enough. A company may value tradition... but if the world is no longer interested in video cassette tapes or Victorian style tables then that business is going *out* of business. Alternatively, if the marketplace is moving online and cheaper, it makes a high-street shop selling the same thing more of a niche/luxury market.

This is also true at an individual level. We need to keep our skills current even though we may need to maintain our old skills too. To stay ready is to keep moving!

In terms of adaptability, consider the following exercise. Write down all the things you enjoy about your job; the things that give you meaning and motivation. For each item, you could also write down why (i.e. what does that give you)? This list is part of your 'psychological work contract' (i.e. beyond the formal contract of payment, terms/conditions etc.) As an aside, you could apply the same questioning process to other areas of life too (e.g. house/home, relationship, friendships etc).

When you have established your psychological contract (or 'criteria'), look at each criterion in turn: what would be your reaction if a change removed that from your list? Depending on the criterion, you might have a range of reactions from "not bothered" through to "I'm off"!

I would suggest that one of the reasons people get nervous about change (beyond the unknown and uncertainty) is the fear of losing something from their list… even if they don't consciously know what their list is!

So, to alleviate the worry or concern about what we might lose from a change, you could do the following:

- By writing your list (and hence bringing it to your awareness), you can look at alternative ways of meeting the needs on your psychological contract. For example, if you like the social aspect but you are no longer working with a team, who else could you socialise with? Where could you socialise in a way that would be meaningful to you?
- In effect, how can you maintain what is good/important from the old (by adapting) *and* get the benefits from the new?
- Remember, change tends to bring about gain as well as loss. What is or could be good about the 'new'? What are the potential benefits?

This thinking process will help you to regain control in times of change… and get back in the driving seat, no matter what curves and bumps there are on the road ahead.

To focus on what is within your control… 20
To model how nature deals with change… 29
Or continue to predicting change…

120. Predicting Change

One of the best ways of coping with change is to expect it. If you see a change coming, it does not have the same 'surprise' shock value. People who are less affected by change tend to live in the now but also keep an eye on possible futures.

Some futures that come to pass are relatively easy to predict. Climate change, for example, will (depending on where you live in the world) bring with it more extreme weather patterns and faster flora/fauna changes. In the UK, on average, it will no doubt be warmer (hence less snow… not good if you are a sledge maker), rainier (hence more flooding), stronger winds (more risk of damage), infestations of non-native species (e.g. 'new' insects affecting the ecosystem, crop damage etc.) Now of course, it is easy to be pessimistic about the future, but use this moment of pessimism to help you predict and plan for the worst. Let it constructively inform you in your decision making. For example, don't buy a house near a flood plain or river… buy one on a hill!

If you want to be prepared and well informed, choose your sources of information wisely. Newspapers and social media are not a great source of credible information (as they are opinion/politically based… and biased). 'New Scientist' magazine is a better source, with credible articles, based on research… and an easy read (and no, I do not work for them!)

Play the 'future forecasting' game from time to time:

1. Consider how the world might be different in 5-10 years' time. Think about the following areas: technology, working/living environments, social, fashion, financial, global environment, political etc. What might we have, see, do, experience that is different?
2. If these things are true:
    - What impact might that have on your sector?
    - How will your company need to be different in order to exist in that new world?
    - How might your job and working conditions be different?
    - How could this affect your role and the priorities in your role?
    - How might this affect your personal priorities?

Predicting change means keeping a view on the bigger picture of time. What are the threads of the past and the present… and how might they weave into possible futures? And how will you deal with those possible futures?

Expect change… predict it and plan accordingly!

To get into a state of readiness… 14
To focus on big picture thinking… 82
Or continue to psychological reactions…

121. Psychological Reactions to Crisis & Change

When we are going through a crisis or significant change, we tend to experience a range of reactions over a period of time. The same is true with a sudden change that we feel is happening 'to' us… particularly when we did not see it coming and we can do nothing to stop it.

The following 'Change Ladder' is designed to give you an idea of some of the reactions we might have. We start at the bottom and then move upwards:

6. Application	Getting on with it. Changes are integrated. Implementing the **new** 'business as usual'.
5. Adaptation	Creativity and innovation. Developing ideas as to how to 'be' in this new reality and how to tackle the challenges of the situation.
4. Acceptance	Coming to terms with the reality of the situation. Resilience strategies begin to kick in. Closing the 'fantasy-reality gap'. "It is what it is."
3. Awareness	Understanding that there is a new situation/problem but feeling e.g. anxious/ frustrated/depressed/overwhelmed.
2. Avoidance	Also known as denial. Avoid thinking about it, acting or taking it seriously. "It'll never happen (to me)."
1. Affliction	External stimulus generates an initial impact/shock. Breaks us out of our 'norm'.

This model is an adaptation of the classic 'change curve'. The reason for adapting the original is to show the loops of reactions that people go through during times of crisis. Rarely do we experience a logical step-by-step progression through the stages. We might flip from anger to proactivity to mild depression to anxiety to brainstorming ideas to taking action to feeling frustrated etc. This is linked to what is known as the 'hope-disillusionment' cycle.

Of course, when faced with a specific, reactive, emergency-crisis (e.g. an accident or a split water tank), we tend to act immediately (or freeze or want to run away). However, in terms of handling a longer-term crisis, this model describes the layers of psychological reactions.

It is important to realise that you are not unusual or abnormal for bouncing/looping around.

To shift how you see the change…39
To find a moment of calmness and inner peace… 46
Or continue to certain uncertainty…

122. Certain Uncertainty

One of the main issues with change and uncertainty is that we lose the feeling of being 'in control'. It is as if we are sitting in the passenger seat of our own car, waiting for something to happen. In this state, we become a potential victim to other people and our environment.

The feeling of uncertainty can set off a 'threat' mode in the brain, leading to anxiety. This, in turn, can lead to a 'narrow' focus on short term thinking and decision making[i]. The counter to this anxiety and narrow focus is to get curious!

When faced with uncertainty, many individuals freeze up as they don't think they can plan ahead. The following tip is designed to help you practically… and psychologically to feel back in control and 'on top' of things again.

The point is, although we cannot say exactly what will happen, we can take a guess at the likely possibilities.

If you are in a situation where the future is uncertain, start by writing down the range of things that might or could happen, including best and worst-case scenarios. What are the possible future alternatives or the likely consequences of the change?

Then go through each possible alternative one-by-one and write a big-picture action plan of what you would do if this became a reality… "If *x* happens then I will do *a*, if *y* happens then I will do *b* etc."

Also, think about how you could utilise or capitalise on each possible future. How could you benefit from it? In what way might this be an opportunity?

Possible Futures?	**Ideas/Directions?**	**Opportunities?**
If…	*Then I will…*	*How might I capitalise on this?*
a.		
b.		
c.		
d.		
e.		

You should then end up with a list of possible futures, each with a general plan of action associated with it. This helps you to feel back in control of the situation as you are then ready (practically and psychologically) for most eventualities. In addition, if you have noted some opportunities, how could you gain these benefits even if the possible future does not come to pass?

This 'future mapping' approach is designed to give you a sense of reassurance (and anyone else involved in the process), that whatever happens, there will be a way forward.

"Whatever happens, you can handle it."
(Susan Jeffers[ii])

To take control of your confidence… 28
To reassure your inner worrier… 48
Or continue to a lack of direction from others…

123. A Lack of Direction from Others

During your time at work, you will no doubt experience what is known as 'ambiguity' which means, basically, a sense of uncertainty about what is expected of you.

Sadly, not all managers (or management) are brilliant at leading! Some will fail to give you clear structure, outcomes, instructions or priorities when you need these things. Even if they give you the 'what' they may forget to give you (or not know themselves) the 'how'.

If you experience a lack of clarity, direction and/or support from your manager, you have a range of options:

- Wait (like sitting and waiting in the passenger seat of your car)
- Request and wait (at least you have flagged up the issue here)
- Inform your manager of the issue and what you intend to do:
    a) Research (e.g. talk to others, read best practice, search online),
    b) Make a decision based on your research,
    c) Plan your key steps,
    d) Let you manager know what you intend to do,
    e) Take action,
    f) Let your manager know that you have taken action (and if possible, the results of that action).

This may seem like overdoing it for simpler tasks, but you need to remember to keep your manager in the loop. By taking this approach, you are being proactive but not a 'lone-wolf maverick'!

The notion of proactivity in action and communication will also apply to your career development. Do not put your career into the hands of someone else, waiting for them to do something so you can progress. I have heard the frustration in some people's stories where every year at their appraisal, their manager says: "Yes, you are on track," but then nothing changes. Three years later and they are still doing the same job as before… but feeling bitter, resentful, cynical and disliking their manager more and more!

On a smaller scale, the same is true for your learning and development. Do not wait for your manager to find courses for you. Research them yourself and if possible, put a request in. Make it easy for your manager to sign it off by giving them a reason as to how and why the training will help you deliver your job role more effectively.

If you feel your manager is actively blocking your progression, check: are they doing that to others or are you being singled out? If you feel you are being genuinely discriminated against, have a chat with your HR representative.

To remind yourself to get back in the driving seat… 2
To re-assess your career focus… 17
Or continue to a lack of direction from yourself…

124. A Lack of Direction from Yourself

"Arriba-arriba, andele-andele!"
(Get up-get up, let's go-let's go!)

Speedy Gonzales

It is the moments where we feel down or lost that we really test our mettle. When something seems 'insurmountable', we have hit what I call a 'life-challenge'. These are the defining moments where, if you were writing a story about your life, it is time to face a 'dragon' in order to reach your goal.

How you handle demotivation and set-backs will define you. Use the ideas in this book to inspire you… to pick yourself back up again and get focussed:

Ideas for getting back in the driving seat…	**Piece**
Remember that persistence is one of the four keys to success	9
Refocus on what you *can* control.	19
Speak your words of goal motivation (even if it feels untrue to start with).	23
Take the next smallest step.	26
Plug back in to your purpose.	31
If this is part of your story, what path do you choose next?	33
What makes your heart sing?	35
Change your focus… to the things that *are* working.	39
Remember: To bounce-back = to focus on your outcomes.	40
Redirect your brain.	41
Get a dose or two of happy!	42

"Now is the time
to begin to make those things happen…
that one day you will be looking back
and feeling glad you did!"

To refocus and get back in the driving seat, plunge into at least 5 different pieces in this book… and take action!
Or continue to your new job: first impressions….

125. Your New Job: First Impressions

Laying the foundation for progression… it starts on day one of your new job! Now is the time to create the best first impressions you possibly can.

Here are some ideas you might want to consider:

1) **Acclimatise**. Learn about your new job. Explore the company intranet and familiarise yourself with the environment. Walk the floors to see what goes on and where. Smile and introduce yourself where appropriate. Get an organogram/chart to understand the 'map' of the company. Find out what the other departments do. Who are the Heads of Department? If you are not taken on a tour as part of induction, take yourself on one!

2) **Associate**. Frequent the kitchen/coffee area during breaks. Get to know people. Be friendly and become recognisable. If possible, speak to managers more senior than you. Say you have just joined and you are getting to know the business. Ask questions about what they do and what they are working on… and then seek connections. When might you be working with them or their team in the future?

3) **Attend**. If you are a senior manager, go to relevant meetings and get to know colleagues. Go for walkabouts. Be seen. Get to know others around the business. Chat to people. Find out what is challenging as well as rewarding and working well.

4) **Act**. Do your job and do it the best of your ability. Establish who can help you when you don't know something. Seek to

return favours. If you are a manager of a team, introduce yourself and tell them what you will be doing over the first few weeks. For example, working with and having 1:1s with individuals. This will give you a sense of any historical issues. Then hold a team meeting to discuss the future and everybody's expectations. Resolve issues where you can but avoid changing things just for the sake of it!

Good luck and be brilliant!

After Word

When you meet Destiny at the crossroads,
make sure that you are ready.

And by the way, give her my regards!

Love, learn and enjoy…

Notes, Further Reading & References

2 **The Driving Seat**

i) At cause vs at effect is used in the NLP field to denote being responsible for your own state vs being a victim/at the mercy of/making others responsible for your state. If I ask you: "Who is responsible for your behaviour?" I hope you would answer that you are responsible for your own behaviour. If I asked: "Who is responsible for your thoughts?" I hope that (despite the possible effect of media and influential people in your life) you would acknowledge that you are. Finally: "Who is responsible for your feelings?" Again, we are each responsible for our own feelings. And yet we often want to blame others… "they upset me"/ "they make me so angry" etc. When we blame others for how we feel, we are handing control of our emotions over to someone else!

ii) Reacting vs Responding. I don't know who initially noted that the 'ability to respond' is to take 'responsibility' for your actions, but it is pretty well used now. What I find more interesting is the basis of each word: 'react' is to reactivate, like a knee jerk reaction...

stimulus ➔ behaviour,

whereas 'respond' implies a thought process in the middle (as in 'ponder' – consider, reflect)...

stimulus ➔ thought ➔ behaviour.

3 **The Resilient Career**

i) Life challenges can happen to anyone at any time. I call these things 'critical unforeseen events' (*CUE points* – a term I also use in project management). A snowstorm or flu outbreak can be a CUE point, preventing us from doing something. When an event involves sudden unexpected costs, a friend of mine calls this '*random tax*' (and very occasionally we might also get a 'random rebate'... an unexpected windfall). The point is... it is not personal, so don't treat it as such. Even if it is a person that affects your life, treat them as a random snowstorm. To feel resentful and angry with someone for what they have done to us will only injure *us*.

ii) Resilient: from Latin *resilientem* 'inclined to leap or spring back'; from *salire* 'to jump'. Also links to the words 'result' (the consequence or rebound) and 'salient' (prominent).

iii) Growth mindset: the belief that we *can* change and develop. See "*Mindset*" by Carol Dweck (2017).

6 **Credibility**

i) "The person who is the most certain is likely to be the most persuasive." I first heard Tony Robbins use this phrase in one of his audios; I cannot remember which but it stuck in my mind.

7 **Connection and Credibility**

i) This comes from research by Ellen Langer in her book "*The Power of Mindful Learning*" (1998).

ii) First Impressions: it takes a 2 second judgement to determine a person's competence, confidence & honesty (Nalini Ambady & Robert Rosenthal, "Thin Slices of Expressive Behavior as Predictors of Interpersonal Consequences: A Meta-Analysis", *Psychological Bulletin* 1992, Vol. 111, No. 2, 256-274). Seeing a photo of a face for 1 second (and comparing to others) gave people enough time to predict the winner of an election AND the margin of victory. This was later demonstrated as taking a tenth of a second (according to article in *New Scientist* 01.10.16). Unfortunately, this can also make us prejudicial against people. Here are some more research examples:

Time It Takes	**What We Judge**	**Reference**
50 Milliseconds	Extroversion: How outgoing someone is	bit.ly/PMExtroversion
100 Ms	Competence, Trustworthiness & Likeability	bit.ly/PMFirstimpressions
10 seconds	Neuroticism: Seeing someone walk, neurotic or adventurous?	Bit.ly/PMGaitCues
1 minute	Potential for Success: From facial expressions: competence and leadership capabilities	Bit.ly/PMFacesSuccess
5 minutes	Social status: what wearing? Social standing and earning potential	Bit.ly/PMClothingImpressions

15 minutes	Hire or not hire?	Bit.ly/PMHiringDecisions

8 **Flexibility**

i) This phrase is an adaptation of W Ross Ashby's 'Law of Requisite Variety'. It was borrowed from the cybernetics field into the Neuro-linguistic Programming field. "*An Introduction to Cybernetics*", by Ross Ashby, (1956)

10 **The Persistence/Flexibility Combo**

i) An interesting book about 'neural plasticity': "*The Brain That Changes Itself: Stories of Personal Triumph from the Frontiers of Brain Science*" by Norman Doidge (2008).

ii) When out of work, make finding your next job your *new* interim job. Create a routine of networking, connecting with HR folk in your industry, contacting, updating your CV to the values of each company, registering with recruitment agencies and online notifications. Do some voluntary work relevant to your field/skills (but don't over-commit). This may all sound obvious… the trick is to remain persistent and flexible.

11 **Is Success About Being Lucky**

i) 50% down to luck? (Donna Lu, *New Scientist* – 05.10.19, p15)

ii) See "*The Luck Factor: The Scientific Study of the Lucky Mind*" by Richard Wiseman (2004).

iii) Luck requires passion, perseverance, imagination, intellectual curiosity, and openness to experience (Scott Barry Kaufman, *American Scientist*, March 2018)

12 **Meet You at the Crossroads!**

i) Seneca, 1st century Roman philosopher must be one of the earliest to refer to luck being at a crossroads.

17 **Where is Your Career Focus?**
i) The idea for introducing the step: 'Remedy' (between problem and outcome) comes from the 'PRO' model by James Lawley and Penny Tompkins: https://www.cleanlanguage.co.uk/PRO.html

20 **Out of Control: Into Control**
i) This is explored in more detail in "Solving Impossible Problems 2nd Ed" by Joe Cheal (2020).

22 **Those That Achieve Goals & Those That Do not**
i) 'Well-formed outcomes' is a model you will find in the NLP (neuro-linguistic programming) field. The acronym 'POISED' is our version of the model.

ii) The SMART model has been around for many years. For your interest, here is the original paper published about it: Doran, G. T. (1981). There's a S.M.A.R.T. way to write management's goals and objectives. *Management Review*, Volume 70, Issue 11, pp. 35-36.

24 **When Goals Seem Out of Reach**
i) For more information about the performance formula, see: *"The Inner Game of Work: Focus, Learning, Pleasure, and Mobility in the Workplace"* by W. Timothy Gallwey (2001).

26 **The Destination is in the Journey!**
i) 'End state energy is introduced in an audio *"Beyond Goals"* by John Overdurf (2004), www.johnoverdurf.com

ii) I started writing a number of books many years ago… but didn't complete them. The 'next smallest step' approach combined with the joy of completing another book helps me to keep it going. As an aside, the other thing I learnt about writing a book is that you tend to go through about 5-7 drafts of writing, editing, rewriting, reformatting etc. I have a philosophy when writing: love it, hate it, love it… i.e. love writing it, be your own biggest critic when reviewing/editing it, then love it again as you make it even better!

27 **Do Some Modelling!**
i) Modelling is at the core of NLP (neuro-linguistic programming).

32 **…the Purpose of Being**
i) "Every problem has a gift for you in its hands", from *"Illusions: Adventures of a Reluctant Messiah"* Richard Bach (1989)

34 **Understand Your Values**
i) You will also find that for every context, you will have a 'hierarchy of values'. For example, what is important to you about your career? Write a list. Then compare the items on your list and decide which is the most important. Go through each: "Which is more important X or Y?" until you end up with a prioritised list.

36 **Finding Good Company**
i) Whilst there is no such thing as a 'perfect' organisation (or type of organisation), you may be able to find the *best fit* for you. Your decision will also need to be based on the leadership/ management styles within a specific company and the way things are run. Here are some general pros and cons of the four organisational drivers, orientations and focii:

	Stakeholder Oriented	**Cause Oriented**
Results Focus	• Pros: Financially rewarding, competitive, exciting. • Cons: Lack of welfare, wellbeing and work-life balance. You are only valuable if you are performing. Can be cut-throat/ruthless.	• Pros: Making a difference, feel-good factor. Part of a movement and working with people who have similar beliefs/values. • Cons: Cause can become an excuse for pressure and bullying (you are either with us or against us, if you believe in the cause, you'll stay late). Some charities can be well-intended but without business skills… i.e. disorganised! They expect everyone else to believe in the cause.
	Staff Oriented	**Customer Oriented**
Relationship Focus	• Pros: Feel supported, nurtured and cared for. Development opportunities. Staff satisfaction, happiness and wellbeing. Engagement. • Cons: Can be 'over-nurturing' (smothering in cotton wool). Less individual responsibility. Everyone too 'nice' to get be assertive, make difficult decisions and get the job done on time. Conflict avoidance.	• Pros: Happy customer is a customer more likely to return. Mistakes taken seriously. Responsive to the market. Use feedback and complaints to improve systems. • Cons: As customer service improves, customer expectations rise… a never-ending cycle. Hard to please all the people all the time. If the customer is always right, where does that leave an aggrieved member of staff?
	'Internal' Priority'	**'External' Priority**

37 **Understand Your Belief Bubble**

i) Jean Piaget suggested that children go through two phases as they develop their schemata ('belief bubble' or 'internal map of the world'). The first is *accommodation* where they consistently change/update their schemata to fit new information coming in. As the schemata become coherent (and hence 'set'), the child then turns the process on its head by shifting to *assimilation*, which means changing the information as it comes in to fit the existing schemata (and ultimately *world view*). Adults will tend to *assimilate* (or ignore) information that does not fit their world view unless they are forced to *accommodate*.

Our belief bubble is a necessary part of our survival. It helps us to predict outcomes, learn more efficiently and function more effectively in new situations. However, if our bubble becomes too rigid, it can lead us to be narrow minded, inflexible, intransigent and intolerant of other perspectives. If we think of it as our 'internal map of the world', when the map is fixed, there may be a fear of anything beyond the map… a fear of the unknown… '*hic sunt dracones*'… 'here be dragons!'

We build our bubble to survive and so it becomes critically important to us as individuals. Perhaps our bubble becomes intrinsically linked to our sense of identity. And hence, if someone or something threatens our bubble, it could feel as if our very life is on the line. And so, we defend our bubble, at times to an extreme (e.g. crusading and warring against others who have different maps to us). More often (i.e. on a day to day basis) we defend our bubble psychologically, perhaps by filtering what we experience and then manipulating those experiences.

ii) The deletion/distortion filters are part of the 'meta-model' from NLP (neuro-linguistic programming). What I call the 'belief bubble' is a collection of 'generalisations' we make about ourselves, others, the world (the way it is and the way it should be). This is also known as our map or model of the world. We could say that what we delete and what we distort is **driven** by our generalisations. In turn, deletions/deleting and distortions/distorting **protect** the generalisations and hence help to **maintain** them. If generalisations are the central core and then deletions and distortions are 'lines of defence', we might imagine the following simple and yet dynamic model:

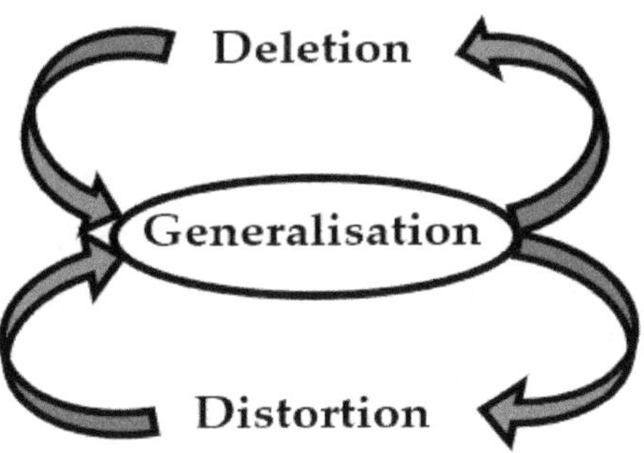

38 **Understand Your Bias**

i) If you want to explore and understand more about your own bias, have a look online at the 'Implicit Association Tests' on the Harvard University website: *https://implicit.harvard.edu/implicit/uk/*
Also see: "*Sway: Unravelling Unconscious Bias*" by Pragya Agarwal (2020)

ii) For a more details of gender bias language and a list of masculine and feminine words, go to:

- *https://newtonsoftware.com/blog/2016/12/22/gender-discrimination-in-job-descriptions/*
- http://gender-decoder.katmatfield.com/

39 **How do you see the world?**

i) You cannot necessarily change someone else's perspective/ position, but you can say "So that's your experience of X, and my experience is Y." This is (a) hard to argue with and (b) invites them to see the world from another perspective. Sometimes it is useful to help a person realise that what they perceive *is* a perspective and not **the** 'truth'.

40 **Resilience is Fundamental…**
i) For example: http://www.litrejections.com/best-sellers-initially-rejected/

42 **Give Your Brain a Dose of Happy!**
i) According to research in 2018, a bath can be as good as physical exercise for improving depression and sleep patterns. (https://www.newscientist.com/article/2183250-hot-baths-could-improve-depression-as-much-as-physical-exercise/)

44 **Wonderfully Unwonderful!**
i) For an in-depth exploration into meta-states, see "*Meta-States: Mastering the higher levels of your mind*" by L. Michael Hall (2012).

45 **Be Mindful of Your Choices**
i) For the most profound example of 'choice', see "*Man's Search for Meaning*" by Viktor Frankl (2004).

46 **The Zero Point**
i) The Zero Point model was originally inspired by the works of Eckhart Tolle (e.g. his book "*The Power of Now*" (2003) and various audio recordings). The Zero Point model is not designed to be a summary of his ideas, but I wanted to acknowledge and recommend his work.

47 **What to do with the 'Inner Critic'**
i) For more about the daydreaming and the default mode network, see Catherine de Lange's article, 'Superdoodles: The science of scribbling', *New Scientist* (18.12.12)

49 **The Landscape of Experience**

i) Writing down how you feel: there is a useful technique from 'positive psychology' in distancing ourselves from a negative experience: write down what happened and how you felt. Emotions have their own form of logic, an '***emotilogic***' as it were. They need to be acknowledged, labelled and expressed... otherwise they tend to rattle around inside and can eventually manifest as physical tension. For this, I developed the ALE acronym as a reminder to myself to acknowledge that I am feeling something, label it (i.e. say what the emotion is, even it is a mix) and then express it by writing it down or telling a third-party what happened and how I felt. If you want to develop your emotional labels, search for '*Plutchik wheel*' online.

50 **Seeking Feedback**

i) As an aside... out of nearly 2000 people surveyed, 'Cheers' ranked as 4th worst email sign-off after 'love', no signoff and 'warmly'. Apparently, they preferred: 'kind regards', 'thanks' and 'regards.' Smiley faces were 12th in the list of general 'don'ts' (though I do tend to use these with folks I have rapport with). In terms of greetings, people liked: 'hi', 'good morning/afternoon', 'hello' and 'dear'.

Article: "The most IRRITATING email lingo revealed" 09.01.20 https://www.hrgrapevine.com/content/article/2020-01-09-are-writing-the-most-annoying-things-in-work-emails?utm_source=template-pardot&utm_medium=email&utm_campaign=hr-09-01-20&utm_content=news&utm_term=Communication (accessed: 07/08/2020)

51 **Self-Disclosure**

i) For more information about self-disclosure as a personal development tool, have a look online for the Johari Window. E.g. https://www.communicationtheory.org/the-johari-window-model/

53 **Put on Your Presenter Shoes!**
i) See *"The Model Presenter"* by Joe and Melody Cheal (2013).

55 **Close the Gap: Get Connected**
i) See *"The Model Presenter"* by Joe and Melody Cheal (2013).

ii) Alan Pease, Honorary Professor of Psychology at ULIM International University, Author of Body Language: https://www.youtube.com/watch?v=ZZZ7k8cMA-4

58 **Prepare to Persuade**
i) The WEB model is also useful for negotiations. 'Worst' is also known as your 'walk-away-position' (i.e. that you will not or cannot go above or below). In order to have a 'walk-away', you need a 'back-up plan' to walk away to. If you have no back-up plan, you have no walk-away-position… and hence no limit on your 'Worst'. (This would be bad news!) To determine your 'Best', as long as you can justify asking for it (e.g. with a 'because…'), then you can start there. You might not get your best, but it is where you plant your starting 'flag in the sand'.

61 **How to Get A Salary Increase**
i) A survey in August 2020 (just at the start of a 'deep recession' caused by the Covid19 pandemic) suggested that 40% of total respondents expected to get a pay rise in the next 12 months. In the 25-34 year-old bracket, it was an optimistic 60%. This unrealistic expectation (particularly during a time of unprecedented chaos) is an example of a 'fantasy-reality gap' and *might* even be described as an 'entitlement fantasy'. The survey was carried out by CV Library (and at the time of writing this book, this is an interesting website for career related articles: https://www.cv-library.co.uk/career-advice/)

64 **How to Get Realistic… About Time**
i) See *"Who Stole My Pie?"* by Joe Cheal (2014)

67 **Why Do Some People Not Progress?**
i) See *"Empowering Yourself"* by Harvey Colman (2010). I am not sure where this percentage comes from, but Coleman refers to it in his book. He uses the terms: Performance, Image and Exposure.

71 **Your Brand Awareness**
i) This phrase is a shortened version of a more famous quote: "Speak when you are angry and you will make the best speech you will ever regret". This appears to be attributed to Groucho Marks. https://quoteinvestigator.com/2014/05/17/angry-speech/

77 **Spontaneous Confidence When Put 'On the Spot'**
i) See *"The Model Presenter"* by Joe and Melody Cheal (2013).

78 **Addressing Imposter Syndrome**
i) I confess that this is a bit of an educated guess, based on observations of and feedback from more than 500 presenters over a 25-year period.

79 **Your Online Presence**
i) a natural 'real' smile is known as a Duchenne smile where the corner of your eyes 'crinkle' as well as the mouth smiling. The easiest way to achieve this is to find something to laugh, chuckle or chortle about (although you might want to avoid guffawing).

84 **Being Seen and Heard in Meetings**
i) You can often determine the 'psychological' leader of a group by noticing:

- Who do others in the group match/copy/mimic (e.g. body language, postures, facial expressions)?
- Who does the group agree with most often (through verbal and non-verbal means)?

- Who do some folks look to just before they go ahead and speak, or who do they address directly instead of the whole group?
- Who do people pay most attention to?

87 **Be the Positive Force for Change**
i) If you do need to complain at some point e.g. for poor service, here's a quick strategy: Explain what has happened (the problem) and the impact it had. Say that you are obviously not happy. Then *ask them* what they can do to put things right… (It may not always get you a result, but it's one of the easiest approaches I've found to date.)

ii) These four factors (Acknowledgement, Acceptance, Appreciation and Admiration) are based on our 'levels of trust' model that we discuss more fully in *"The Relationship Dance"* by Joe and Melody Cheal (2018). This model was designed as a counter-set to John Gottman's Four Horsemen of the Apocalypse of relationships (stonewalling, defensiveness, criticism and contempt… see, for example, *"Why Marriages Succeed or Fail"* (2007) or *"The Seven Principles that Make Marriages Work"* (2018) by John Gottman)

88 **Connectivity: The 'Right People'**
i) I originally learnt about this kind of idea from an influential business woman, Tricia Cusden. She called it a 'powernet'. (Her website now is https://www.lookfabulousforever.com/)

101 **Networking: Why and Wherefore**
i) Inspired by Malcolm Gladwell's Mavens, Connectors and Salespersons (in *The Tipping Point* - 2002).

107 **How to Dissolve Career and Life Dilemmas**
i) See *"Solving Impossible Problems 2nd Ed"* by Joe Cheal (2020) for more details of the Dilemma Integration Technique (DIT). If you

use the DIT for a specific dilemma, but find you are still stuck, here are some more methods for moving on:

1) If there are only a *limited amount of answers* (or limited from one side) ask "And what else does that give you?"
2) Look at anything *still conflicting* in the mix and for each of the conflicting items ask: "What does that give you?" writing the responses in place of the conflicting words.
3) Look for any *material/tangible* items on the list (e.g. a Ferrari) or anything to do with *other people* and ask: "What does that give you?" writing the responses in place of the old words.
4) Look for any *negations* ('not' words – e.g. 'not stressed'). Ask: "If you weren't being/doing/having that, what would you be/do/have?" Replace the words on the page.
5) Look for any *judgements* (e.g. good job) or *comparisons* (e.g. better house) and ask: "What does that give you?" writing the responses in place of the conflicting words.

108 **Effects of Success on Work-Life Balance**

i) See "*The Paradox of Success*" by John R. O'Neil (1994)

109 **Being Prepared for Success**

i) Another benefit of understanding the role above you (if you are seeking to move up a level) is to manage your expectations. Your manager's role may not be as easy as it initially appears. Get to know the job description plus all the extras (including have to cover for the level above them). Be prepared for the psychological responsibility. The more senior you get, the more you have to translate external 'volatility, uncertainty, complexity and ambiguity' (VUCA) into a workable business plan. It is like being a parent… your kids think you know everything (as you thought about your own parents), but the reality is, you have to figure it out as you go along!

110 **Not Enough Time**
i) See *"Who Stole My Pie?"* by Joe Cheal (2014)

111 **Dealing with Pressure**
i) This phrase comes from *"Feel the Fear and Do It Anyway"* by Susan Jeffers (1987). I use it a lot as a reassurance statement for resilience during times of uncertainty. It is as near a 'truism' as you can get. The point is, no matter what has happened in your life... you have handled it. It may not be exactly how you wanted to handle it... but you did. The evidence? You are here now... reading this book.

112 **Working From Home**
i) If you can meet up with people face to face, or visit the office regularly, so much the better. This allows you to have more 'shared experience' with colleagues, to have 'random conversations' and build the 'weaker' links in your network (which are also good for your wellbeing). Being in the office space increases your 'social capital' (your ability to get and share resources with others, including 'emotional' support, sharing of ideas and practical help). People with greater 'social capital' tend to: have better physical and mental health (including wellbeing/resilience), perform better, feel more engaged (e.g. in a community), find work more easily, collaborate better, feel a greater sense of belonging and laugh more! For more about 'social capital', see the article: "Missed Connections" by David Robson, New Scientist 15.08.20.

113 **Not Sleeping Well?**
i) I would recommend reading something like: *"The Power of Now"* by Eckhart Tolle (2003).

115 **It's Not Me... (Oh Dear! Maybe It Is Me!)**
i) I first learnt about the psychological version of 'family of origin' from Julie Hay during a Transactional Analysis (TA)

workshop (although it dates back to at least the early 1980s). If you are interested in an accessible book on business TA, I would recommend her book: *"Working It Out at Work"* (2019)

116 **Dealing with Difficult Behaviours**

i) For a fascinating book on the topic of psychopaths and sociopaths in the workplace, see: "Snakes in Suits: When psychopaths go to work" by Paul Babiak and Robert D. Hare (2007)

ii) When dealing with angry outbursts, you might be dealing with 'now' emotions (stimulation) where someone feels e.g. unjustly treated in the current moment. Alternatively, you might be dealing with 'historical' emotions (re-stimulation) that don't always seem to make sense to those around (and sometimes the reaction appears 'over the top' for the situation). When anger is historical, it is usually driven by fear, which in turn is driven by an old hurt. There is a saying from the 1950s… 'hurt people' hurt people, i.e. those that carry historical hurts tend to lash out at others.

117 **How to Handle Conflict**

i) See *"Solving Impossible Problems 2nd Ed"* by Joe Cheal (2020). There is a chapter on managing disagreement and conflict, and the whole book is about approaches to handling tensions and polarities.

122 **Certain Uncertainty**

i) This desire to simplify and seek clarity during times of volatility, uncertainty, complexity and ambiguity (VUCA) is known as 'certainty addiction'.

ii) See *"Feel the Fear and Do It Anyway"* by Susan Jeffers (1987)

Index

About the Author

Joe Cheal

Joe is the Lead Imaginarian and Facilitator for Imaginarium Learning & Development. He has been involved in the field of management and organisational development since 1993. In focusing his training, executive coaching and consultancy experience within the business environment, he has worked with a broad range of organisational cultures, helping thousands of people revolutionise the way they work with others.

He holds an MSc in Organisational Development and Neuro Linguistic Technologies (his MSc dissertation was an exploration into 'social paradox'), a degree in Philosophy and Psychology and diplomas in Coaching and Psychotherapy.

Joe is an NLP Master Trainer who enjoys learning new things... by exploring diverse fields of science, philosophy and psychology and then integrating these 'learnings'. He is the author of *'Solving Impossible Problems 2nd Ed', 'Who Stole My Pie?'* and the co-author of *'The Little Book of Persuasion (Updated)', 'The Little Book of Resilience', 'The Model Presenter' and 'The Relationship Dance.'* He is also the creator and editor of the *Powered By NLP* series and the NLP Journal: *Acuity.*

Imaginarium Learning & Development is a consultancy that specialises in inspiring the natural potential of organisations, leadership, management and individuals through OD, L&D and Executive Coaching.

We work with clients from a broad range of sectors and aim to work in partnership with our clients, enhancing the profile of leadership, learning and development in our client's organisation.

Since 1993 we have experience of working with thousands of people from many organisations including:

Abcam, Adoption UK, Aeroflex, Amnesty International. ARA (Aircraft Research Association), Association of Local Councils, Astra Zeneca & AstraTech, Autoglass (Belron), Avondale. Balfour Beatty (Haden Young), Bardsley England, Bedford Borough Council, Bedfordshire County Council, Beds Health, Beds Magistrates Courts Committee, Berry Gardens, BGP Products, Bio-Products Laboratories (BPL), Birdlife and Plantlife, Bodleian Library and Ashmolean Museum, British Broadcasting Company (BBC), BT, Calderdale Council, Cambridge City Council, Cambridge University Libraries, Cambridge University Press, Camelot, Canon UK & Europe, Canterbury Christ Church University, Cardtronic, Cellnet, Central Bedfordshire Council, Children's Trust (Tadworth), Church Conservation Trust, Cognita Schools, Cranfield University, Dixons Stores Group International, Elizabeth Finn Homes, Emmaus Village Carlton, GSK, Halton Foodservices, Hertfordshire County Council, Herts Magistrates Courts Committee, Hertsmere Borough Council, Illumina, Innovative Trials, Institute of Cancer Research, Institute of Engineering and Technology (IET), J Murphy & Sons, Kentec, Langley Search & Selection, Legal & General, Lockheed Martin, London Borough of Camden, Luton Borough Council, MCA, Mercedes AMG Performance Powertrains Ltd, Mid Beds District Council, Mr Plant Hire, Mylan Pharma, Newham LA, NHS, North Herts District Council, OAG, Olympic Blinds, Porthaven Care Homes, RSPB, RSPCA, Sainsbury's, Santander, Serco, Shepherd Stubbs Recruitment, Signature Senior Lifestyle, St. Alban's District Council, Staverton Park Conference Centre, Stevenage Leisure, Sussex Wildlife Trust, Team Domenica, Teignbridge District Council, Tesco, The Assessment Network, The Wine Society, Three Rivers District Council, TOPRA, Tunbridge Wells Borough Council, University of Hertfordshire, University of Limerick, University of Kent, University of Sussex, Wealden District Council, Welwyn Hatfield Borough Council, Welwyn Hatfield Community Housing Trust, Willmott Dixon, World Animal Protection.

Imaginarium offers a range of consultancy services including:

- Learning & development / training courses
- Executive coaching and skills coaching
- Facilitation and team development
- Change management and organisational development
- Strategic engineering and paradox management
- Myers Briggs profiling and emotional intelligence testing

Our courses and topics include:

LEADERSHIP DEVELOPMENT
Change Management
Coaching Performance
Delegate!
Feedback for Effectiveness
Making Meetings Work
Management Development Programmes
Managing People Successfully
Mentor Skills
Motivate!
Project Leadership
Team Building and Development

RESULTS AND RELATIONSHIPS
Assertiveness: Clarity and Focus
Building Partnerships
Communication
Conflict Resolution
Customer Care
Dealing with Aggression
Dealing with Difficult People
Handling Conflict in Meetings
Influence and Persuasion
Magic of Mediation
Negotiation Skills
Understanding Personalities

IN FRONT OF THE AUDIENCE
Advanced Presentation Skills
The Essential Presenter
Persuasive Presentations
Train the Trainer

PERSONAL IMPACT
Career & Profile Development
Coping with Change
Dealing With Pressure
Innovation: Getting Creative
Managing Your Performance
Resilience: The 'Bounce Back' Factor
Staying Positively Happy
Stress Management
Time Management
Understanding Unconscious Bias
Wellbeing: Psychological health

EXECUTIVE DEVELOPMENT
Advanced Negotiation Skills
Becoming a Mentor
Beyond Selling
Making NLP Work
Managing Tensions
Organisational Development
Organisational Politics
Storytelling in Business
Strategic Change Management
Troubleshooting: Problem Resolution
Working with Transactional Analysis

HR SKILLS FOR MANAGERS
Appraisal
Capability & Disciplinary
Controlling Absence
Dealing with Poor Performance
Introduction to Counselling
Managing Difficult People
Recruitment Selection & Interviewing
Tackling Bullying & Harassment

Why work with Imaginarium?

Here are 4 things that make us special…

Experience

Imagine tapping into a wellspring of experience to help your people become more effective, more efficient and even more resourceful.

We have been involved in the learning & development environment for a quarter of a century! In the training and coaching environment, we have encountered and understood the majority of problems and challenges that human beings can face. We are able to draw from a wealth of practical resources, solutions, examples, models, hints, tips and ideas to help get people unstuck (and to help them 'unstick' themselves!) As individuals, we continue to learn and develop, keeping what we do fresh and engaging. We 'get' people!

Credibility

Imagine working with a company who regard your success and credibility as highly as their own.

We value not only our own credibility but also the credibility of the company we work with. We know that when we are training and coaching in your company, we represent "learning & development". We are passionate about advancing the reputation and culture of people development in organisations. We have worked with a vast range of organisational sectors and cultures giving us the ability to adapt from one company to another. We have also worked with some highly multicultural organisations, from people from all across the globe.

Humour & Enjoyment

Imagine your staff… keen to develop themselves to become even better at what they do.

We love what we do! People who train with us enjoy themselves. We've been told that some people laugh and smile more in one day than they normally do in a week! We believe that enjoyment and light-heartedness are one of the most important keys to learning. Wherever we have embedded into an organisation's culture, people want to attend courses!

Return on Investment

Imagine working with people who care that their service adds measurable value.

It is important to us that whatever we do, it adds value for your company. Sometimes this can be realised in terms of financial profits and savings. Sometimes return on investment is subtler in terms of staff motivation, efficiency and improved communication. Whether the returns are tangible or intangible we are keen to make sure that we are worth our weight in gold!

Psychological Approaches to Coaching Diploma

Accredited by the Association for Coaching

The programme is designed to allow learners time to reflect, consolidate and practice between modules. Each module is three days in length and includes supervised coaching practice with feedback.

For experienced coaches there is the opportunity to dip into the programme and attend individual modules. As this course is accredited by the Association for Coaches the modules can be used as CPD.

The modules are:

- Foundations in Coaching
- Transactional Analysis for Coaches
- Using the iNLP Coaching frame work
- Positive Psychology Coaching

Other Books from GWiz Publishing

SOLVING IMPOSSIBLE PROBLEMS
Second Edition

By Joe Cheal

Say goodbye to organisational dilemmas, tensions, conflicts and stress with ***Solving Impossible Problems****.*

The ability to manage tensions, paradox and uncertainty in business is becoming a much sought-after leadership skill. 'Paradox Management' is a new but increasingly essential field in the area of business management and will be highly influential in the ongoing sanity and success of all organisations and of the people who work for them.

Solving Impossible Problems will give you a greater understanding of organisational tensions and paradox. You will learn how to recognise these 'twisty turny' problems and then use practical tools to resolve them or use them for innovation.

This book is a unique guide to heightened wellbeing and enhanced thinking power through the revolutionary process of ***Paradox Management****.*

Other Books from GWiz Publishing

WHO STOLE MY PIE?

By Joe Cheal

How to manage priorities, boundaries and expectations

Walter's lunch... and his time are being eaten into.

Fortunately, 'real-world' help is at hand to help him manage his time... and inadvertently, his pies!

Join Walter in learning how to manage priorities, boundaries and expectations...

Make your life easier and more fulfilling!

Who Stole My Pie is packed with powerfully simple models, tools, tips and techniques. If you want to gain greater control over your time then this book is for you!

Other Books from GWiz Publishing

the

MODEL *presenter*

By Joe & Melody Cheal

The Model Presenter will show you how to:
- Develop the qualities of an exceptional presenter
- Create a memorable and logical structure
- Deliver presentations and training with confidence.
- Engage an audience easily and effortlessly
- Deal with a wide range of challenging situations

This 'how-to' guide is filled with steps to follow and helpful hints and tips modelled on the best of the best.

You will discover a host of original material including:
* Closing the Gap between yourself and the Mind of the Audience
* Preparing using the BROADCAST Model
* Delivering training sessions using the IMPACT Formula
* Transforming nerves into confidence

Be remembered for the right reasons…
*As you become **the Model Presenter**!*

Other Books from GWiz Publishing

THE LITTLE BOOK OF RESILIENCE

By Joe & Melody Cheal

Develop your Resilience skills!

The Little Book of Resilience is full of practical tools, tips and techniques
that will help you to…

Bounce Back from Life's Challenges
Get Back in the Driving Seat
Shift Your Perspective - The Way You See It
Discover More Meaning, Purpose & Wellbeing
Change How You Feel

Other Books from GWiz Publishing

THE LITTLE BOOK OF PERSUASION

UPDATED

By Joe & Melody Cheal

If you were more persuasive...

What would your life be like?
Where might you be and what might you have?
Where could you go and what could you achieve?

The Little Book of Persuasion is bursting with practical idea for using anywhere. Build relationships and get better results at home, at work and out in the big wide world!

Other Books from GWiz Publishing

The Relationship Dance

How would your life be, if you and your partner were always on the same side… facing life's challenges together?

A relationship is a dynamic pattern of advancing and retreating 'energies'. A *healthy* relationship is a graceful dance of balanced and constructive interactions. Indeed, the quality of your life is determined by the health of your relationships.

The Relationship Dance is a guide for anyone who wants to improve their ability to relate, communicate and share happiness and meaning with a loved one!

In this book, you will discover how to:

- Create a solid foundation with the *Five Relationship Graces*
- Remain *balanced* and *constructive,* even when you face differences
- 'Clean up your own act' to develop a healthy and rewarding relationship
- Build and maintain a *complementary* and *interdependent* relationship
- Communicate assertively and *speak your truth with kindness*
- Revivify that 'honeymoon feeling'

Other Books from GWiz Publishing

Becoming Happy!

Lessons from Nature

By Melody Cheal

The search for happiness can often seem elusive and so this book provides hope for those wanting help in becoming happy. Find out how to unlock the best version of you, recognising your own sense of worth and value. Melody shares experiences from her own journey of self-discovery plus tools and ideas she uses in her own practice.

The combination of pictures drawn from nature plus simple easy to apply exercises provides the reader with tools to begin transformation.

Are you ready to Be Brilliant?

For more information about
Joe & Melody Cheal,
Imaginarium Learning & Development
and/or GWiz NLP,
you can contact us at:

E: info@imaginariumdev.com
E: info@gwiznlp.com

Ph: 01892 309205

W: www.imaginariumdev.com
W: www.gwizNLP.com